WE ARE THE

99%

AND WE ARE RUNNING FOR OFFICE

WE ARE THE

99%

AND WE ARE RUNNING FOR OFFICE

WASHINGTON'S WORST NIGHTMARE

LARRY FRITZLAN

RWP Recovery Works Publishers

Copyright 2012 Larry Fritzlan

Published by

RWP Recovery Works Publishers

21 Tamal Vista Blvd., Suite 226
Corte Madera, CA 94925

Cover and text design: *the*BookDesigners

Note: This book contains substantial excerpts from *Intervention on America*
by Larry Fritzlan (Recovery Works Publishers, 2011).

ISBN: 978-0-9847573-3-6

First Printing, March 2012

I dedicate this book to my grandchildren, Loren and Elijah, and to all children, whom we must all serve. I also dedicate this book to Jackie, Erik, Camille, Jack, Kate, Erik, Killyan, Andrew, Sam, Scarlette and Kelsey. Each day I cheer as you courageously take your place as adults in an uncertain world.

ACKNOWLEDGEMENTS

We each depend on so many people as we aspire to fulfill our dreams and reach our potential.

It would take volumes to acknowledge those who have helped me up to the next step or over the next hurdle, or who have held me as I integrated the swirling world inside and all around me, from my birth to this moment.

My teachers and mentors. Michael Kahn, Jon Vander Zwaag, Stephanie Brown, Brant Cortright, Carolyn Foster, Judye Hess, Steven Bosky, Tim Cermak, Rick Lavine, and Jack Kornfeld. Your wisdom has inspired me and challenged me. This book and my work are indebted to your generosity.

Leslie Keenan has held my hand and shepherded this project from my first written outburst to completion. Leslie, thank you. You are the Godmother of this book.

Julia McNeal, wizard with the pencil who created order to my writing. Thank you so much for your wisdom.

To Katy Butler, Nita Gage, and Carolyn Foster. You are the wise writers who have inspired me and modeled for me what successful writing looks like.

To my colleagues Bill Arigi, Jennifer Graham, Mary Beth McClure, Russell Hendlin, Stephanie Daigre, Paul Marra, and Richard Lipfield. On a daily basis we put our heads together in hope that we are making the right decisions in our work with our clients.

What would our world be without the journalists and others who broadcast their unique perspectives to all of us? There are too many to list them all, but some readily come to mind: Tom Friedman, Peggy Noonan, Frank Rich, Chris Hedges, Charles

Krauthammer, David Carr, and Bret Stephens. And I must add Jon Stewart and Stephan Colbert, whose humor and satire portray reality in stark relief.

My son David and his family, especially my grandchildren, Loren and Elijah. It is their future that has compelled me to push this book forward.

And my wife Avis Rumney, without whom this book would not have been written. Thank you for your endless love and support. Your wise counsel, tireless editing and encouragement have made this book possible. Each day I marvel at what we have accomplished and daily wonder what our next adventure will be. I love you so.

CONTENTS

The true essence of humankind is kindness. There are other qualities which come from education or knowledge, but it is essential, if one wishes to be a genuine human being and impart satisfying meaning to one's existence, to have a good heart.

— THE DALAI LAMA

INTRODUCTION

90% of Americans are angry at Congress and yet we can predict that we will send most of the same congresspersons back to serve again! And again, and again.

We may be angry with Congress, but who sends our representatives to Washington?

We do.

In my book, *Intervention On America*, I point out the inconvenient reality that we Americans (you and I) are not fully sane. We have, slowly, over time, been inducted into a dysfunctional system, and it is *we* who enable, we who vote for, and we who send back to Washington the same lying and corrupt officials. *Over and over!* It is we who are failing to see the reality that it is *we*, and not *they*, who need to change!

It is we who must wake up to the solution that is right in front of us. We have been confronted over and over again with the same corrupt Democrat or the same corrupt Republican who "sweet talked" us or "scared" us or "bribed" us to keep sending them back to Washington. Our politicians' endless election campaigns require massive amounts of money that corporations and the hyper-wealthy gladly supply, in exchange for special breaks from their regulators – an unethical, dual relationship that favors both parties, at the expense of Americans. Greed, money, power, and influence have corrupted our elected officials, whose behavior more closely resembles that of oppositional 14-year-olds than that of adults

What can we do? If over 90% of us are distrustful of our elected officials, why haven't we actually fixed the problem?

Most of us have been asleep. We fall for the Party Line. We socialize with like-minded left- or right-leaning folks. We continue to identify with a Progressive or a Conservative mindset, failing to see that the underlying system itself is what's broken. Our current system consists of politicians who believe that they must raise huge amounts of money to pay for ads. They get their cash from the 1%, but it has strings attached, strings that benefit the 1%, almost always at the expense of America's vitality.

We can't grumble about what is wrong with Washington and then claim that "our guy" is somehow immune to the corruption that is hardwired into all parts of Washington's politics.

For instance, Obama, in spite of his rhetoric, has put his hand out and received more money from Wall Street than have all the Republican candidates combined! His re-election campaign already has over $1 billion! They are all on the take. *Your* elected official is on the take. It has been estimated that the typical politician in Congress spends 30 to 70% of his time begging, extorting, or trading access to power, for money. Please go to www.opensecrets.org and see the money *your* politician has accepted from Big Business, Big Union, Big Lawyer, Big Pharmaceutical, Big Transportation, Big Tobacco, Big Food, Big Health Insurance, Big Military, Big Media and the hyper-wealthy. They are, with only a very few exceptions, all on the take. Seriously, go to the Web and see for yourself.

It's not the liberals or the conservatives who are the problem. It is the *system* that continues to produce a class of politicians who will prioritize moneyed interests and their party's interests over common-sense solutions to the big problems we face today.

I'm proposing a way out. I'm proposing a simple fix. I'm proposing a solution that changes the system itself. A solution that eliminates the perpetual quest for money to run endless campaigns.

I agree with the Tea Party Movement. Doesn't every sane American realize that we must balance our books? And I agree that Washington is bloated and needs reorganization. The Department of Agriculture, for example, is in charge of a food policy that costs taxpayers 14 billion dollars, and whose corruption has led to a government-mandated food policy that will result in one out of every three babies born after 2000 developing diabetes! We actually would be better off if we eliminated most of the Department of Agriculture *and* got rid of the politicians who support this sickening process.

I agree with the Occupy Wall Street Movement. Wall Street bought off our elected officials to water down the regulations that protect us. These dishonorable Americans on Wall Street gambled with our money and bankrupted us. During the Depression, in the 1930s, in a moment of sanity, Washington created laws, such as the Glass-Steagall Act, to protect us. But slowly, due to Washington's and Wall Street's greed and endless quest for more money, tragically, these protections have been removed, and the American taxpayer has been ripped off.

And I agree with those who want to mount a Third-Party Movement. Both the Democratic and Republican parties are so sickeningly out of touch with America that we are desperate for something, even though Third-Party Movements rarely change the system.

I see a fourth way.

I see a way that includes the best of the Tea Party Movement, the best of the Occupy Wall Street Movement, and the goals of the Third-Party Movement.

As I see it, the solution to our problem is simple. We ask everyone running for office to sign the following pledge:

The Money Out of Politics Pledge

"I agree to accept no money from any corporation, lobby, PAC, or entity other than a person, and I agree to accept no more than $100 from any individual."

That's it. If they don't agree, we don't vote for them. We only vote for those who sign the pledge.

If we held every current politician in office to this standard, we would have to replace all 537 of them (1 President, 1 Vice President, 100 Senators, 435 Representatives). They have all been on the take! In order to acquire the money they needed to get elected, they have had to be longtime, established members of the Club (Democrat or Republican). In order to get re-elected, they needed to spend the majority of their time in Washington trolling for cash, which they've been given in return for doling out special favors. *Taking cash from someone you regulate is an unethical, dual relationship.* It is wrong, and it happens all the time in Washington.

The Internet provides an immediate, free, and comprehensive

way for any politician to communicate a position, a platform, and a plan. Most Americans have Internet access today. YouTube videos can convey vast amounts of information – it was a YouTube video on Facebook that encouraged Egyptians to meet in Tahrir Square in January 2011. No longer is it necessary for a campaign to rely on expensive newspaper, television, and radio ads. By using the technology at our fingertips, we can campaign today, for a fraction of what it has cost in the past.

I love America, and its history and its greatness. I love our Constitution. It has held this democracy together, with all its flaws, for over 200 years. I am grateful that we have law and order. No civilization can endure without it. And I have supported our two-party system. The Republicans stand for strong, responsible, and independent individuals, and responsible local government. Who could not be for that? And the Democrats favor our coming together to care for the young, the old, and the disabled, and for using our collective wisdom to protect Mother Nature. Who could not be for that?

Ultimately, we will need a constitutional amendment to codify a sane election process that completely removes money from elections. Will the process include publicly funded elections, like many countries have, or something else? This will have to be worked out, but it cannot happen today because everyone who is currently serving, from Obama on down, has been bought off. Those who are serving cannot turn their backs on the very system they depend on for survival.

A number of years ago, Congress made an attempt to pass sane election laws but, as Harvard law professor Lawrence Lessig points out in his book, *Republic, Lost: How Money Corrupts Congress – and a Plan to Stop It*, there were 25 lobbyists from the 1%, corporations, and the hyper-wealthy *fighting against* change, for every lobbyist working *for* an ethical, fair, and sane election policy. The moneyed interests, the less than 1% who control the reins of power, will fight, tooth and nail, to keep power.

The current system is *locked up, solidly in place and unwilling to change.* If change is to occur, it must start with us.

The politicians have sold their souls to the 1%. In order to keep power, they continue to go along with the Party Line.

This book is a How-To Manual for updating our political system. It is a How-To Manual for creating a political system that we can trust. Such a system would encourage bright Americans with sane vision to enter politics. We need honorable candidates on the ballot, honorable Republicans and honorable Democrats, Americans who agree not to accept money. And those new candidates have to be us. You and me. Only when we have the option to vote for someone who is not bought by the 1%, will there be the possibility of electing new and honorable leaders.

Please, dream big. The majority of Americans are looking for new leaders. 65% of Americans are sympathetic with the Occupy Wall Street Movement. Nearly all of us can understand the Tea Party's anger at Washington's failure to balance its budget. And both parties have been so inept that most of us would love for some third party to come to the rescue.

There is a huge vacuum. We don't trust Washington because our leaders are not honorable!

Everyone – left, right, and center – is looking for sane, grown-up, honorable leaders to meet the challenges facing our country.

We have been here before. We were here in the 1770s, and we came together, stood up, and created America. We got the job done and created this nation. We were here in the 1940s, and we came together and got the job done: we defeated Hitler. Today is similar. We are in a crisis, and our current leaders can't even punch their way out of a wet paper bag!

The world is in a state of rapid change. If we use our intelligence, we can initiate an amazing future. And if we continue to stay in denial, we could destroy our planet. Big changes are coming – one way or another, our future will look much different from our current situation. The reality of a new paradigm unfolding is inevitable.

Disruption is now the norm.

The Big Question is: "Will we choose to use our intelligence to usher in a sane and sustainable future that protects children, nature, and future generations, or will we choose to stay in denial, ravage the planet, stress our children, and roll on toward the inescapable crisis?"

You and I cannot avoid making this decision. Not acting *is* a decision!

We are at a nodal point in history, and we all need to step up again and serve. We all need to put down the plow and go to the Town Center and support our new leaders. We need to do this, or we need to accept the reality that one-third of babies born today will develop diabetes, greenhouse gas emissions will increase, our bankrupt economy will continue its downward trajectory, Wall Street will continue to gamble with taxpayers' money, and your elected officials will continue to accept bribes from the 1%, and lie to us.

An article in the *New York Times* on December 27, 2011, reported that the net worth of U.S. Senators and Representatives has gone up in recent years while the net worth of most Americans has gone down. Why? Among other reasons, "loose ethics controls, members' shrewd stock picks, profitable land deals, and favorable tax laws." There it is! (http://www.nytimes.com/2011/12/27/us/politics/economic-slide-took-a-detour-at-capitol-hill.html?pagewanted=1&ref=politics)

For my part, I have decided to run for the U.S. Congress from my local district, California's new, 2nd Congressional District. I pledge to fight like hell to support a complete overhaul of our election finance system. We need to get money out of politics, and we need to elect an entirely new slate of officials who have a hopeful view of America's future. New Democrats and new Republicans. And then we need to roll up our sleeves and restore sanity to our country. We need leaders who inspire us to greatness.

We need leaders of this type and caliber at every level of government – city, county, and state, as well as federal.

Part One of this book delineates the reality of our current election system. It helps the reader come out of denial and become willing to act. Then it provides a solution (The Money Out of Politics Pledge) and presents an argument to counteract the hopelessness that many succumb to when believing nothing can change.

I have visited my local elections office and I have begun the process to get on the Democratic primary ballot as Representative for California's 2nd Congressional District. I will do my best to win, and I will go to Washington and stand up for sanity.

Part Two of this book is my vision for America and my agenda, which can be summarized simply as follows:

1. Restore democracy by getting money out of politics.
2. Restore Mother Nature.
3. End the Drug War.
4. Serve the children.

Many of the principles that support my agenda were introduced in my previous book, *Intervention On America*. I reiterate them here, and include substantial portions of the text relating to them from that book as well, because they are my vision of what our government needs to do to restore our country, our people, and our planet to health and sanity.

The premise of my previous book is that the American political system resembles an alcoholic family system in need of an Intervention. Our leaders, part of the 1%, behave like addicts. Their craving for power and money is out of control. Their behavior has adversely impacted all of us, for decades. I believe that 20% of Americans (40 million voters), left, right, and center, are sane enough to initiate this Intervention on the 1%. I proposed in my previous book that these forty million American voters go to the streets once a month and initiate our own American Spring that will lead to democratically replacing the "bought off" politicians in Washington and enacting campaign finance reform. We really can have an amazing future!

I pledge to join you on the Washington Mall or at my Town Center or at a similar gathering place every month until this madness stops and we have restored sanity to our democratic process.

We can do this. We just need to come out of denial and realize that we can. We can get money out of politics, use the democratic process to elect honorable, inspiring, non-moneyed leaders, and join with our new leaders to restore sanity to our nation.

Let's do it!

PART ONE

1

COMING OUT OF DENIAL

We have slipped into denial. We want to believe we have sane leaders. We want to think that they will do the right thing. We hear their words and promises and we want to trust them. We can't believe that they are all mentally disordered, because of what it would say about us, the folks who elected them. How could we elect leaders who were not very sane unless we were not very sane ourselves?

Denial, as psychologists remind us, is a defense mechanism that our ego uses to protect us from unpleasant feelings. It is a condition in which the mind makes things up that are not real.

A person in denial cannot tell the difference between reality and fantasy. We have all been amazed when someone who obviously is an alcoholic informs us that they "don't have a drinking problem." Clearly, they are not sane. Clearly they are "making things up."

I make my living working with people in denial. I'm a Licensed Family Therapist who specializes in intervening with and treating families suffering from addiction. Individuals who are living with addiction are not fully sane. They are living with an insane person, and their lives lack love, joy, and serenity. They have contorted their lives to fit the craziness of addiction, and they can't see the insanity in their midst. No one in the system knows what "getting a life" means. They don't have a clue about "high-level wellness."

Here is what we are in denial about: Our leaders are not leading. The future of our planet is at stake, and our leaders are ignoring some very grim realities. They continue to prioritize their own self-interests over the health of the planet, our country, our citizens, and even children.

We are faced with serious problems. Here are a few:

- Massive corruption. Every single federally elected official has accepted cash from corporations and the hyper-wealthy, to rig the system in favor of the wealthiest 1%.

- Global warming, which threatens the entire planet. We don't even have an energy policy in place.

- Environmental degradation. Wildlife, rivers, and the Amazon rainforests are being destroyed – our soil and air are rapidly becoming depleted and polluted.

- A massive rip-off of the American people by Wall Street. This rip-off happened when Wall Street gave our federal officials money to rig the system in their favor. No one has gone to jail for this.

- Collusion between our elected leaders and Big Food – the companies that produce mega amounts of chemically-altered, nutrient-deficient, food-like substances – resulting in the production of food that is so bad that our children's generation will not live as long as their parents' generation.

Why is this so? Why are our political leaders missing the obvious? They are like the captain of the Titanic, oblivious to the danger ahead. I believe that nearly every citizen knows we have a problem, but no one has been able to coherently articulate it and then come up with a plan to address it.

Just like an alcoholic promises to fix the mess he has created, these elected leaders promised us that *this* time it would be different. And yet they continue to work out backroom deals, rigging the system to get re-elected.

And we see that nearly every single elected official, both on the left and on the right, has sold out America to those who fund their elections. We have seen how special interests, corporations, and the hyper-wealthy, have purchased their special tax deals and subsidies and protections and lucrative contracts. We have seen how this oligarchy, less than 1% of America, hold the levers of power and dictate the agenda for the rest of us. And how this agenda is bankrupting us, killing our children, and putting our planet at risk. We see their *loss of control* over protecting their self-interests at the cost of the nation's well-being. We see their *craving* for "more," at the expense of sanity. We see the *adverse consequences of their behavior* all around us. And, their behavior is *chronic*. Those who comprise the 1% have always seen to it that they got more and kept more than the majority of U.S. citizens.

"We shall require a substantially new manner of thinking if mankind is to survive."

— ALBERT EINSTEIN

But I see the best in us, and I wish to disprove Einstein's view that we will destroy ourselves. Primatologist Franz De Waal's brilliant work, I believe, illustrates the core question that humans face. Did we evolve from the often-murderous, patriarchal Chimpanzee, or did we evolve from the loving, matriarchal Bonobo? The history of the world has many examples of both forces at work. We have seen angry Americans who are highly defended and seem ready to strike. Children raised in these homes are exposed to objectifying, egocentric talk of "us vs. them" and "the enemy." The adults in these homes allow their children to be exposed to violence, killing, and separation. There are also many American communities where children grow up and see adults lovingly interacting, warmly embracing, peacefully celebrating, and diligently protecting them from violence and negativity.

Much of America's, and the world's, past, has been about power, ego, greed, and "me." This stance has led to amazing wealth (billionaires), amazing accomplishments (men on the moon), and amazing minds (Einstein, the Dalai Lama, Steve Jobs). It has also led to a world where billionaires fly in their private, carbon-burning jets, while many of their brothers and sisters starve to death, below. This approach has led to 1% of Americans setting in motion forces that could drive our country into bankruptcy, and the planet into mass extinction.

We have reached a point in our evolution where we are ready for a new political paradigm. What passes for grown-up political parties today is a joke, and anyone who is awake knows it. We can do better. These elected officials have brought us to the edge of financial collapse, runaway spending, high taxes, terrorism, unworkable healthcare plans, toxic food, environmental damage, crowded prisons, homelessness, joblessness, and the destruction of our children's future. They rig the system so that our only choice is to vote for them over and over again – or, not vote. In June 2011, one pundit said it might already be too late to run alternative candidates on November 6, 2012 – 17 months before the election!

We have been watching the Arab Spring Uprisings bring down corrupt governments. It is time for our American Spring uprising. It is time for America to recover the moral high ground. As a country, we need to peacefully go to the streets, and let our officials in Washington know that we see their game, and we are done with it. Even if there *are* honest politicians, they need to sit on the bench for a few innings. Collectively, all 537 of them have failed. They did not get the job done. Common sense answers to big problems have eluded them. Wouldn't it be great to *recall and replace all of them in this coming election cycle?*

Almost everyone wants change. This is one thing that both the right and the left can agree on. Almost everyone is looking for an answer.

Let's start with something we can all agree on.

We want children to be cared for. We want loving families. We want peace and tranquility in our lives. We want to live in balance with Mother Nature. We want our chosen leaders to guide us wisely. We want institutions that will protect us when things go wrong.

And almost all of us can agree with the Declaration of Independence:

"We hold these truths to be self-evident, that all men are created equal, that they are endowed by their Creator with certain inalienable Rights, that among these are Life, Liberty and the pursuit of Happiness."

No one among us would dispute this. We could poll all the current presidential candidates, and they would all agree on this.

So, what happened?

Recent polls show that over 90% of Americans are unhappy

with the way our current leaders are managing the country. And we are disgusted at the enormous funds politicians somehow acquire and spend to get re-elected. How did Obama get a *billion* dollars?

For example, politicians use our tax dollars to subsidize the production of high fructose corn syrup in order to get kickbacks from Big Food, and then use that money to support their election campaigns so they can remain in their positions.

Our elected leaders and those who run Big Business are endlessly looking for a "fix." They are compelled to seek "more." They need "bigger and better." "Economic growth" is their religion. They exhibit *greed* in their continual quest for power, money, and material wealth. Their greed, their endless quest for more, has become an unquenchable monstrosity that literally is destroying our planet.

The 1% don't mind spending a little of their profit to get the right people elected. This is how they can ensure that they will continue to get the special favors and tax breaks they've come to rely on.

The system perpetuates itself, and the 1% continues to wield the power and the influence. But they haven't attained this position of privilege single-handedly – they are aided and abetted by us, the voters. You and I, and every other American citizen of voting age; we are the individuals who have been enabling our government to operate this way by choosing to re-elect these leaders. *We, the citizens of America, voted these men and women into office. And we, the citizens of America, have not fired them!*

I am responsible for this mess. And so are you. Left, right, and center. If change is to occur, we need to start with this truth. We can no longer stand around in denial, like drunks at 2 a.m. arguing with each other. We need to sober up. We need to start with the reality that it is we, ourselves, who created this unmanageable mess. Once we accept that reality, we can change. And then, we can elect ethical and moral adults to replace our current leaders in Washington.

It is vital to understand that you and I are supporting this dysfunctional system. *We* are enabling our current mess. Here's how we did it, and continue to do it:

1. We voted for a Democrat or a Republican (it doesn't matter which, they are both engaged in selling access to power).

2. We passively stood aside and did not vote.

3. We chose not to stand up against them (not marching, not throwing tea in the river, not writing a book, not blogging, etc.).

4. We fell for the old trap of trying to "work from within the system." (Something that *rarely ever* works in an addictive system).

In *Intervention On America*, I offered an analogy between an alcoholic family system and our current dysfunctional political system. Briefly, I explained that it is next to hopeless for the members of an alcoholic family system to perform an intervention on themselves. Similarly, it is just as hopeless for those who are now in office, and those on the left or on the right, to fix America's current government. With an addicted family, we know that the addict is in denial of his addiction and is not sane. But the codependent-enablers are also in denial of how their very behavior actually supports and perpetuates the status quo. They simply cannot have an objective view of the system as a whole and of the complex and convoluted interrelationships of the individuals in the system. The same holds true of our political system – it cannot be fixed from within, because no one on the inside can grasp the enormity of the dysfunction or see a way out.

In an addicted family, everyone might think that he or she can change. The codependent-enablers endlessly try one thing after another with the hope that the addict will change – but things only get worse. And the addict endlessly believes that he will get control of his addiction, but he never does. It is only when an interventionist steps in from outside the system and guides the family into a new paradigm that real change is possible.

Many individuals and groups, left and right, are trying to fix our system, believing that replacing a few leaders will do the trick. I believe this approach is hopeless, because every one of our politicians knows they need money from the 1% to get elected. They have become addicted to cash and power and will never give those up. Ever! The only way to get sanity is to *change the system* by voting in leaders who pledge not to accept money from any business or corporation, but only from individuals, and only in amounts of $100 or less.

And, just like the codependent-enablers in an addicted family, it turns out that even the sanest 20% of us are also in denial. We may grumble, but most of us have not yet put on our shoes and gone to the streets or written a book or a blog.

If you feel you're in that Sane 20%, as I believe I am, it's time to wake up. We, you and I, need to come out of denial and see that we, the sanest among us, have actively or passively enabled the current mess and that we need to make a decision to actually do something to change the course of events, before it is too late.

There are many myths we have come to believe, myths that politicians use to convince us that the status quo is fine. "Hydrocarbon Extraction" is one such myth. According to this myth, we can extract more and more oil, gas, and coal from the earth to supply our ever-increasing energy needs. The myth is that we can increase the rate of extraction indefinitely to create the "endless economic growth" our current political leaders and Big Business seek in their unquenchable craving for "more."

The Hydrocarbon Extraction myth began with the industrial revolution. We extracted carbon from the earth, ignited it to warm things up and make wheels go round. As time went on, we developed better tools and machines to reach deeper into the earth's crust. We got better and better at extracting carbon and found more and more ways to burn it. We moved into the desert and burned carbon to cool the air in our homes. Cars got bigger and bigger and burned more and more carbon. The pace of extraction accelerated, and the rate of carbon use increased. Then China, India, Brazil, and other countries began to outpace America with their voracious need to burn even more carbon.

From NASA:

> "Human activities add a worldwide average of almost 1.4 metric tons of carbon per person per year to the atmosphere. Before industrialization, the concentration of carbon dioxide in the atmosphere was about 280 parts per million. By 1958, the concentration of carbon dioxide had increased to around 315 parts per million, and by 2007, it had risen to about 383 parts per million. These increases were due almost entirely to human activity." (http://www.nasa.gov/mission_pages/oco/news/oco-20090113.html)

People who are sane and paying attention are aware of the myth that we've been fed by those with power and influence. If the Hydrocarbon Extraction myth of infinite energy supply is not challenged, we might face a future where we will have dug up all the carbon, burned it all, killed Mother Nature, and created a planet too hot to sustain life, killing all of us.

This is not sane.

But our elected officials obviously believe that the carbon supply is infinite and burning it will not impact the planet, even though the evidence of global warming has been pouring in for years. Their denial and refusal to accept the truth is reflected in the absurd reality that oblivious officials and their Big Business enablers have utterly and completely failed to come up with *any* energy plan! "Full speed ahead and damn the torpedoes!" *Not sane!*

President Obama, in his recent State of the Union speech, said that we have "enough natural gas to last a hundred years." OK, and then what? Do we think of the untold generations that will follow us? Do we wonder if they might like to have some to use? Those of us who are not in denial were sickened by his words.

We need to find a saner group to lead us. We need leaders who are not in denial. We need leaders who are wise, and who act like adults.

I believe the Sane 20% among us are capable of coming out of denial. I believe that we can restore the country to sanity. But first, we must come out of denial ourselves, face reality, and be ready to act.

We are the ones who can change what's happening, and we must begin to visualize how we can bring this about.

Most Americans are enablers. While many are very troubled and upset, the majority of Americans neither fully grasp the unfolding horror show nor have a clue about the radical steps necessary to bring about fundamental change. The majority of the electorate will grumble, but will vote to re-elect President Obama or vote for the Republican candidate for President. They will re-elect most of the current Senators and nearly 100% of the Representatives, even though over 90% of the voting public thinks all of them do a crappy job.

(There it is, America! We think they are nincompoops, and yet we send them back!)

These frightened and confused Americans, the majority, are the ones we must talk to. They won't vote for new Senators and Representatives – or they won't vote – because they don't think it will make a difference. They don't see that they are actually contributing to the problem.

We need to educate these enablers about their role in perpetuating our unfolding disaster. They are scared, hurt, and angry. We see them, the strident on the left and on the right. We see them on cable TV, hear them on the radio, and read their blogs. They are making a lot of noise because they, too, are very frightened for America.

The sane and aware among us need to calmly but actively invite the others to join us. And almost all of them will come, because they are fed up with the insanity too, and are hungry for leaders who are honorable. They will eventually see the wisdom of what this means for them and for America. This has been my experience when intervening with addicted family systems – in time, generally everyone gets on board and there's a positive outcome.

We Americans have inherited more wealth and abundance than mankind has ever known. And, we have, in the blink of an eye, watched as our country has "hit bottom." We inherited a Rolls Royce and are in danger of driving it off a cliff in a drunken stupor.

Chief Seattle, the revered and honored Native American Suquamish Indian Chief, in 1854 reminded us that we need to protect the earth for the next seven generations. Of course we need to do that. Actually, we need to protect our planet for forever. But look at our oil use. The Artic icecap is melting, polar bears are drowning, the permafrost is thawing, and the decision by President Obama and the Democrats and the Republicans to keep on drilling and fracking makes every one of the Sane 20% weep.

Is there hope? Think about this:

Democrats and Republicans, like all of us, are amazed at what we Americans were able to do between December 7, 1941 and September 2, 1945, Japan's formal surrender and the end of World War II. We got focused, united around a purpose, built hundreds of thousands of ships, planes, tanks, trucks, and everything else that was needed to stop tyranny and create peace in Europe and Japan.

We rationed gas. We rationed food. Everyone pitched in. *And in less than four years, we completed our mission.* We created democracy and freedom where it had not existed.

We can do the same with renewable energy.

Today we have the technology to shut down the coal burning,

mercury-spewing, carbon-emitting, planet-warming, electricity-generating coal industry. We could install wind generators and solar-powered generators and shut down these coal-burning plants. Industry, science, and technology have shown us that *we could have done this decades ago!*

If we think about what we did in World War II, we can see that this would be simple. We can see that we could do this in just a year or two – if we had the vision, the unity, and the will. If we had another "Sputnik Moment."

Jeremy Rifkin, in his just-released book, *The Third Industrial Revolution,* clearly points out the amazing opportunity a new paradigm could offer us. He writes that Americans, sadly, "continue to be in a state of denial, not wishing to acknowledge that the economic system that served us so well in the past is now on life support." But he offers us an obvious solution if we are sane enough to "get it." He seems to be saying that we have a simple choice. We can blindly continue down a path toward disaster or wake up and embrace an amazing new paradigm.

Sadly, we have elected Republicans who've been bought off by the coal producers, and we have elected Democrats who've been bought off by the coal workers' union. These corrupt elected officials have been bribed to protect the status quo. This information is readily available. They don't deny accepting the cash. This dishonorable and corrupt behavior has been in the news for years. (It is like living with an alcoholic – we are shocked at first, then we just get numb after awhile.) It is time for us to stop allowing this practice. Is it not obvious that what is happening is wrong and must be changed?

We could intervene with the economy: we could regulate Wall Street's greed. We could do the same with Big Food; food producers and our corrupt elected officials rig the system to push fat, sugar, and salt on our children! We could do the same with our drug problem. And our water problem. And our global warming problem. And our animal and plant extinction problem. And our homelessness problem.

In any of these situations, the Sane 20% could declare, "This has got to stop." I suggest some specific actions relevant to each of these areas in Part Two of this book.

In 1941 we had a problem. We unilaterally identified an enemy. We had leaders with vision. And we had a population that supported these leaders. We all rolled up our sleeves, united, and went to work. We got that job done.

Today, we have a different enemy. Today, the enemy is a dysfunctional political system, coupled with denial. We need leaders with vision and a population that supports these leaders, and we need to unite and go to work to create a solution to this problem.

In reality, there is not a person in America who woke up this morning and said, "Honey, let's vote for the same politicians as before, so they can screw our children (and their children, and all future generations) out of natural resources and ruin the planet! Who cares if our grandchildren live in horror on a dying planet? And who cares if they have to pay huge taxes because we ran up the nation's credit card to the breaking point and then handed the debt to them?"

No one says that. No one means that. And yet, that is what we are doing! *That is what you and I have created!*

Today, in back rooms in Washington, and State Senates and Houses and City Halls all over our country, special interest groups and government officials are "gaming the system." And we continue to allow this.

We will all need to stop "playing victim" and blaming "them." *We put them into office.* We need to take responsibility, grow up, and fix this.

I know life is complex, and the politicians endlessly remind us of this. But we know, in our gut, when something is wrong. Over 90% of Americans are in agreement that what our elected officials in Washington are doing is wrong. The left, the right, and the center agree on this. The "system" is broken. Our leaders have utterly failed to lead. They are like four-year-olds, fighting over which one gets the ball. They are like urban gang members who are more interested in conforming to the party line than in thinking for themselves. They are like crack addicts, lying to get high one more time. They are like the alcoholic who masterfully tells us exactly what we want to hear.

As enablers, we really don't have any control over them. *What we have control over is our actions and ourselves.* We can stand up, vote, and replace all of them. We elected them to serve us and to do a job, but they have failed spectacularly. They must be fired and recalled. All 537. And firing and recalling will not be easy. They have manipulated the system to make sure that they don't have any competition. The current parties may appear to be in opposition to one another, but, in reality, they work very carefully to make sure that no one will threaten their protected status.

> ol·i·gar·chy   [ol-i-gahr-kee]
> *noun, plural* -chies.
>
> 1. a form of government in which all power is vested in a few persons or in a dominant class or clique; government by the few.
>
> 2. a state or organization so ruled.
>
> 3. the persons or class so ruling.
> (Merriam-Webster Dictionary)

Less than one percent of America, fewer than three million individuals, hold the reins of our government. Less than one percent – these three million – the elected officials, the ultra rich, corporations, specials interests – have the power to dictate the entire country's agenda. Less than one percent have manipulated the system in ways that benefit them but will cause the country to spiral into collapse. Those comprising the one percent are not like the honorable leaders we had during World War II. These leaders' self-serving behaviors are perverting democracy, bankrupting our economy, poisoning our children, and destroying the planet. These in the one percent, these three million, control the levers of power, while the other 99% of us stand by and continue to enable this system.

The reign of the 1% must come to an end. We all need to see that America looks more like an oligarchy run by the 1% than like a free democracy.

Each of us will need to change if we are going to change America. And if we change, we can replace our elected officials with sane, adult leaders. But we can only change if we come out of denial. We need to see the insanity of the current oligarchy and replace our current leaders.

All 537 of them. 1 President, 1 Vice President, 100 Senators and 435 Representatives. *Replaced.*

In this book, I am inviting us to dream big. Who will replace these folks? Can we imagine electing men and women who are honorable and do not take money from special interests? Can we imagine electing people with vision who can come up with long-term solutions for what ails America?

Could our next President be you? Actually, it *will* be you. We have no option if we care about our children, our country, and our planet.

I have seen what happens when one person initiates an Intervention, and a whole family goes from the death spiral of addiction to a life of hope and love and fun. Change can happen. But first, you have to believe it is possible.

Every one of us must step up. Just like in World War II, we all need to pitch in.

Being upset and complaining is the dubious luxury of a stable, sane, and safe populace. That's not the world we live in. We are all on the Titanic and we need to re-write that story, or we're going down. The politicians at the helm of the ship don't see this – their eyes are focused on the dollar sign; they are driven by power and greed and the myth of endless growth. The politicians in power are steering our country toward potential catastrophe. They are blind to reality.

This book is not about Republican-bashing or Democrat-bashing, even though both parties are leading us off a cliff. These parties are both like clueless, spoiled brats who are blaming each other for not getting their way

You and I need to imagine taking the reins. Each of us needs to visualize what is possible. And many of us will need to find the courage to lead. I don't want to run for office, but I believe we all have a duty to come out of our denial, stand up, and be ready to serve. Just like in World War II. We need to run for office, locally or at the state or federal level, and we need to work for the campaigns of those we support.

In Part Two of this book, I will propose what I believe is a sane and realistic paradigm for the Republican and Democratic parties. The current parties are not sane, either of them, and we need to simply start over with a completely new cast of individuals.

We voters have been like the codependents in an addictive relationship. We have been hoping that "they" will change. We have begged them to be honest. We have pleaded with them. We have been listening to them for years as they've said, "this time will be different." "Really, this time I promise to regulate Wall Street." "I'm telling you the truth, this time I will come up with an education plan for all children." "Please, I swear I will stop spending money." "OK honey, I promise that this time we will not have any backroom deals,

I will not see those lobbyists." "I swear, I will stop taking bribes from Big Business."

We have been the suckers. Ask the young people. They see that the current crop of leaders is crazy, and that is why many of the youth in our country have given up even caring. And *they* are America's future.

We need to realize that the change starts with me and with you. It needs to start with us.

Many of us were hoping that our elected leaders would change. (They keep saying they will!) But we have seen over the years that the only change is for the worse. The only things we can change are ourselves and our approach.

It is also futile to blame "them." "Blame" is a victim's game. We, the electorate, chose to be in relationship with our elected officials (and the special interest folks who run them). We, the electorate, voted for them, or passively supported the system by not voting. We, the American electorate, chose them. *And now we are freaking out at what we created.*

If things are going to be better, we need to have the courage to change the things we can, which is ourselves. We need to vote, we need to run for office, we need to march, we need to post blogs, we need to tweet, and we need to link up on Facebook.

We need to dump the status quo into the crapper. It will disrupt a lot of entrenched interests. It will devastate folks who are on the take. It will scare those who are accustomed to buying special privileges. And it will terrify every politician, because all of them are about to lose their jobs. *Those of us who are willing to step away from the 1% and their money are Washington's worst nightmare!*

It is we who created this, and it is we who are responsible for changing it. *You and I are the government. They are the 1%, and we are the 99%.*

We need to run for President, for Senator, and for Representative.

If we do not vote for any of the current corrupt leaders, whom will we elect? Who will be our new, sane, adult, and ethical leaders?

The answer is that it will have to be you and I!

Chapter 2 describes a solution to the situation at hand. I envision a simple fix, "The Money Out of Politics Pledge" – a simple and effective path toward financial reform in our elections. It asks that we vote only for honorable, ethical politicians, those who agree to accept no money from any corporation, lobby, PAC or entity other than a person, and agree to accept no more than $100 from any individual.

In order for us to have politicians of this caliber to elect, we need honorable, ethical adults to step up and run for office. Adults like you and me. Chapter 3 is a pep-talk, and a vision for running for office.

2

THE MONEY OUT OF POLITICS PLEDGE

There is the joke that we have all heard, "Do you know how to tell if a politician is lying?" "No, how do you tell if a politician is lying?" "It's easy, their lips are moving and sound is coming out."

I have heard variations of this joke my whole life.

How sad! We could get angry and blame the politicians for lying. This might make us feel better. But then we become the joke! After all, it was we who voted for them! We chose the politicians who lied. We were the ones who put them in office.

This is one perspective.

But perhaps we were doing our best to choose "good enough" politicians, and there is some problem, some process, which causes a good politician to go bad. I believe the problem can be seen from the perspective of ethics and the concept of "dual relationships." We elect our officials to go to Washington to represent us. But what happens is they end up taking cash from the 1%.

Most Americans know in their guts when something is "right" or "wrong."

Corruption is a willingness to act dishonestly in return for money or personal gain. What has led to the corrupt, immoral, and unethical behavior of our leaders – leaders who engage in a dual relationship with those they govern and regulate?

"Legalized bribery has become part of the culture of how this place operates."
– LEON PANETTA

"Almost a hairline's difference separates bribes and contributions."
— RUSSELL B. LONG

"I was participating in a system of legalized bribery. All of it is bribery, every bit of it."
— JACK ABRAMOFF

I believe, as do a great many other people, that the problem is our current electoral system: what we know about candidates and what sways our vote. Throughout history, politicians have needed to let voters know which team they were on (Democrat or Republican or third-party) and where they stood on particular issues. The politicians talked to crowds, large and small. They bought newspaper ads, put signs on lawns, made phone calls, drove people to the polls, and even bribed voters.

Starting in the 1950s, the media began to play a bigger role in this process. TVs allowed politicians to run ads that filled our living rooms with propaganda and programmed our minds to support their positions. The political media consultants' industry was born. Sophisticated marketers used psychology and persuasion to influence the outcome of elections. This practice has expanded to the absurd. President Obama will have a billion dollars in his "war chest" to "sell his story" to us. The opposition will have its billion as well. These folks have found very effective ways to brainwash us. They produce fancy, multimedia TV ads that extol their virtues, and equally high-tech ads that demean their opponents.

How else but as a consequence of current campaign marketing practices do we explain the fact that the American electorate thinks 90% of Congress does a crappy job and yet voters re-elect nearly 100% of the same Congresspersons again? (Please re-read that last sentence.)

"Few things in life are more predictable than the chances of an incumbent member of the U.S. House of Representatives winning reelection. With wide name recognition, and usually an insurmountable advantage in campaign cash, House incumbents typically have little trouble holding onto their seats." http://www.opensecrets.org/bigpicture/reelect.php

Every marketer knows that most buying decisions are made emotionally and justified intellectually. Political "marketers" have mastered ways of playing to our emotions and the unconscious parts of our brains. Our senses take in millions of bits of information every second and we are emotionally, as well as intellectually and rationally, continually altered by this stream of data. Our egos may think we are "in control" and "nothing has changed," but we are affected subtly and repeatedly by what we pay attention to. The hope, of course, is that a wise and educated electorate can use what *Homo sapiens* has that other animals lack – a cognitive, rational, and intelligent pre-frontal cortex that allows us to "think" and "be rational," and not vote based on emotion. But emotion, sadly, often trumps our thinking brain, in politics and in life.

The current electoral system is a joke. It is the polyglot stew of money, media, power, fear, marketing, psychological warfare, emotion, and greed. We can do better. Actually, we must do better. Simple, common-sense answers to big problems are being ignored. We have elected leaders who are frantically trying to get and maintain power and to have access to the cash offered by Big Business, lobbyists, and the hyper-wealthy.

The consequences of politicians' need to do the bidding of those with the money are obvious to anyone who looks backstage where the deals get done. Right now, today, thousands of miners are plundering hilltops in Pennsylvania to get at the coal buried just below the surface. This precious resource is burned throughout the east coast to produce electricity. Burning this coal releases into the atmosphere not only massive amounts of CO_2, a greenhouse gas, but also tons and tons of mercury. Government officials estimate that each year, mercury poisoning damages the nervous systems of millions of children and prematurely kills 4,000 to 11,000 unborn children!

Our "leaders" have to know this – it is in the government's own reports! They know that their own families and their own constituents are being poisoned, and they do nothing. Why? The answer is that they blindly do the bidding of the 1% who themselves, foolishly, can't see past their noses to protect their own children! In many ways, Big Business buys off the Republicans, and Big Union buys off the Democrats.

The dysfunctional relationship between our leaders and those who buy them off is unethical and immoral. We all know that this is wrong.

We naturally are upset when a lone gunman kills innocent people. Or when 4,000 American soldiers are killed in Iraq. But where is the outrage when 100,000 Americans have been killed by mercury in the last decade?

Here's another example of how our current political system is wreaking havoc with the health of American citizens. Obesity has become a national health crisis. Today, some Senator's child is eating food that puts that child at a 33% risk of developing life-threatening diabetes. Why is this happening? Because that Senator's – and his colleagues' – greed caused them to sell out to Big Food's desire for more cash, even at the cost of putting their own children's health at risk! Big Food makes big bucks from selling us fat, salt, sugar – substances that we are genetically programmed to gobble up.

There are simple, common-sense solutions to this problem, but not ones that will ever be approved so long as money is corrupting politics. First, instead of subsidizing the multi-national corporations that produce crap food, small, family-owned, organic farms could be subsidized. Next, we need to acknowledge the tragedy of the insane agricultural policy that has resulted in Americans' addiction to unhealthy food and to the resulting obesity epidemic. (We need to acknowledge this addiction and tax the crap. Right now, your tax dollars go to Big Food, which makes hamburgers at below cost. The reality is that one fast-food hamburger costs our society approximately $25 (the medical costs of obesity, heart disease, cancer, strokes, diabetes, and lost wages). If we taxed sugar, salt, and fat-laden processed food (like we tax tobacco), and subsidized plant-based diets (like organic vegetables, fruits, and whole grains), our taxes would go down, childhood diabetes would almost completely vanish, and obesity would be rare. To those who say that this is "social engineering," I say, bullshit! Our current leaders are massively engaged in brainwashing us and engineering our diets! The 1% spend billions in "social engineering" to fill their coffers.

We need a new way. The current political system is an embarrassment to any thinking voter.

There is another serious flaw in the current electoral system. Due to the arcane structure of the Electoral College, the outcome of federal elections is limited to the results of only a few states and a few districts. We have had national elections in which the guy who gets the most votes actually loses! And we have a crazy scenario in which the citizens of Ohio and those of a few other states are subjected to hundreds of millions of dollars' worth of angry, negative, irreverent propaganda while the presidential candidates skip two thirds of the states because the outcome is already known!

This is how America chooses it leaders!

Then the moment the new teams are chosen, the newly elected folks will immediately scurry about, gathering up cash for the next election!

Urban gangs have a term for admitting new members to the gang. It's called getting "jumped in." It is an initiation process whereby the members beat the crap out of an initiate before he can become a member. Our electoral system is somewhat like this. Once our newly elected politicians get to Washington, they quickly learn the rules. Rule Number One is that you conform to the party line or you will not get money for the next election. But the winners pretty much understand this already. After all, they had to go through a primary election process themselves, and they received lots of cash from both their party and the 1%. They probably already understand the rigged system and have gotten in line. It looks something like this for the newly elected:

> "I, your newly elected politician, agree to comply with the Party Line (Democrat or Republican, not much difference between them) and I will be given cash by the 1%, special interests, corporations and the hyper-wealthy, to fund my Propaganda Machine. I understand that I will be part of a process whereby we (both Dems and Reps) will extract cash from the 1% in exchange for favors. Occasionally, we will remind the 1% that we will rescind their special privileges if they don't kick down the loot to us. Yes, this process has been correctly compared to the Mafia, but we have so brainwashed you Frightened Voters by our slick ads and campaign promises of "better times" that no one really notices, and we can pretty much plan on being sent back to Washington over and over again."

There it is, America. This is what we created! No wonder Rush Limbaugh and the Tea Party are so angry, and no wonder Occupy Wall Street rose up and went to the streets, and no wonder folks at Americans Elect started a third-party movement.

The system is being seen by more and more of us for what it is:

broken, corrupt, ineffective, and insane. Almost everyone is disappointed and wants something better.

I see a fourth way that would meet many of the goals of the Tea Party, the Occupy Wall Street, and the third-party movements.

I call it The Money Out of Politics Pledge.

First, as voters, we acknowledge our intelligence and our right to choose. We refuse to vote for anyone who has been bought. We refuse to vote for anyone who has been or will be bribed (accept money from someone they regulate). We refuse to vote for anyone who sells us out to the 1%. We refuse to vote for anyone who accepts large amounts of cash, whether from a business or a corporation or an individual. Furthermore, we refuse to vote for anyone who campaigns using negative propaganda. We vote only for those who agree to fix this problem. We vote only for those who agree to step away from the 1%. We vote only for those who agree not to play the game the way it has been played. We vote only for those who acknowledge the integrity and intelligence of Americans by conducting only positive campaigns.

The Money Out of Politics Pledge establishes a new class of ethical politicians, honorable adults who agree to not take corporate money or bribes, or align themselves with any group in return for financial backing. These politicians would agree to abide by this pledge:

The Money Out of Politics Pledge

"I agree to accept no money from any corporation, lobby, PAC, or entity other than a person, and I agree to accept no more than $100 from any individual."

I think any rational, ethical, moral politician will easily agree with this. Of course, those engaged in the Massive Voter Brainwashing and Propaganda Machine will go ballistic. Their lifeblood will be removed.

But agreeing with this pledge will not be a problem for any honorable politician. Current Internet technology provides low-cost ways of campaigning. When Senators and Representatives aren't accruing vast wealth by selling votes on the floor of Congress for cash from corporations, politicians can renounce the business of acquiring hefty campaign coffers. I'm running for U.S. Congressman in my local district (California's 2nd Congressional District). And I believe that the new technological world makes it possible for anyone to run for office *and* adhere to The Money Out of Politics Pledge. We Americans can use our noggins and not our guts to choose our leaders.

The Arab Spring was not a campaign-financed event. Gandhi did not inspire Indians to go to the streets and oust England because of a multi-billion dollar campaign. And Martin Luther King, Jr. did not achieve his goals by pandering to the 1%.

The Money Out of Politics Pledge is such a simple solution; many will think it's impossible to implement because they are not acknowledging that we still have the power – the power of the vote.

Even with all the manipulation going on, we actually still have this power, and the 1% know it. That's what they are afraid of. That's why they spend enormous amounts of money – to change your vote or to keep you from voting (because of disgust with the system). But as we saw with Obama's election, and as we saw with the disruption the Tea Party caused, a focused, dedicated group of voters can swing an election, and does make a difference.

My hope is that enough voters will embrace this idea, support the candidates who agree to The Money Out of Politics Pledge, and elect us solely on our vision, ideas, and platforms designed to make America better. And my hope is that other honorable, ethical, adults will use the principles I am suggesting here, and also run for office – whether for the Senate, House of Representatives, Presidency or Vice Presidency. I hope that voters will not vote for anyone who uses slick brainwashing ads to trash opponents. I pledge that I will not engage in negative attack ads, of any kind, on my opponents. And, if in the heat of the moment I slip into negativity, I will publicly make amends for my failure to take the high road. I invite my opponents to do the same.

My platform is outlined both in this book and in *Intervention On America,* and is posted on my website (www.LarryFritzlan ForCongress.com). It is tweeted, and posted on Facebook. My campaign has not, and will not, cost a significant amount of money. I believe that donations of $100 or less from individual supporters will cover my filing fees and campaign costs. My hope is that a sufficient number of voters will be attracted to The Money Out of Politics Pledge candidates and make contributions of $100 or less that will similarly cover the costs of their campaigns.

I look at my Establishment opponents. I see the hundreds of thousands of dollars they have already amassed. I see the Establishment (Democrat or Republican, it does not matter) guys getting in line. I see those who have been anointed by their party. I see the Democratic or Republican or Progressive or Conservative Establishment squirting out the next lock-step gang member ready to comply with the Party Line, and I am aware that whoever they are, they will accept cash from the special interests when they get to Washington. They will get caught in the I-need-mega-money-to-get re elected vortex. It will take time to replace the bought-out politicians and get the system revamped.

Ultimately, we need new laws. We will need to come up with constitutional amendments to rein in the influence of the special interests and the 1%.

If I get to Washington, this will be one of my priorities. Americans have been working on this democracy thing for over two hundred years. Getting money out of politics is simply the next step.

Please help me make this happen.

3

OCCUPY DEMOCRACY – RUN FOR OFFICE!

On December 26, 2011, the conservative publication, *National Review*, featured an article titled: "We Don't Have Our 'A' Team on the Field." It proposed a few ideas for disrupting the Republican primary election process in hopes of getting a more conservative guy on the ticket.

In reality, almost all Americans want a better candidate. With Congress at an approval rating of 10% or less, it would seem that "None of the above" has the inside track for being sent to Washington. Except for one problem.

Only the 1% get to play the game. Or so it has been. Only those who are members of the gang (Republican or Democrat; both parties collude in the election process) are allowed to have any chance of winning.

Or so we have always believed.

This is how it has always been. In every election, I see a Republican, a Democrat, a Green Party candidate, a Peace and Freedom Party candidate, and maybe a few assorted others. The 1% guys (Dems and Reps) always win. They always win because we typically don't think we have another choice. And the smaller parties end up cancelling each other out. And besides, the 1% parties (Dems and Reps) have the money to run expensive TV and newspaper ads.

When I decided to run for Congress, my friends initially thought I was nuts. Then a few of them read my book, *Intervention On*

America, and understood that I was serious. Not only was I serious, but also my platform offered common-sense solutions to many of the problems around us.

Then they said, "You will never win."

The reality is that up until now, they were right; the system was rigged. Only 1%-ers and their bought-off politicians were allowed onto the field. I believe that this is about to change dramatically. The stressors of the deteriorating environment, unstable governments, failed states, wars, overpopulation, technological advances, and collapsing economies are upending countries around the world. 90% of Americans say they do not trust Congress. The Tea Party completely upset a major political party. Occupy folks have been center stage for months and are supported by the majority of Americans. Third-party movements are growing. And even the conservatives are thinking of disrupting their own party's election process by running a new guy!

This is all part of universal discontent that opens the door for new ideas, new leaders, and a new election process.

90% of the lions, tigers, elephants, and whales are gone, wiped out. We are rapidly destroying the Amazon. We are fracking Earth's fragile crust, when we could have stopped using oil and gone sustainable decades ago. Crooked financiers on Wall Street today are gambling with taxpayers' money – they bought off *your* elected officials for this opportunity! Our electoral process does not provide fair representation. More and more of us are coming out of denial and seeing the devastation around us.

Those of us who are upset and who care about our future need to step up. Just like during World War II and the American Revolution. It is time to do that again. It is time for American adults to step up.

Any adult American citizen can run for office. That is what is great about our democracy. America is a nation run by the people: "of the people, by the people, for the people." Our leaders are our humble servants who serve at our pleasure. And we, the people, can replace them when they displease us.

Can you imagine a scenario where every adult in our nation who is concerned about our country and the world actually ran for office? What if thousands of Occupy folks ran for office in districts all over the country? What if the voters in the state primaries had hundreds, even thousands, of Americans from whom to choose? If we distrust the current team of leaders, then we need ethical, honorable folks with good ideas on the ballot whom we can elect in their place.

What a concept: Choosing a politician based on ideas and vision, rather than being limited to two candidates (usually old white men) who have been bought off by the 1%ers.

The scenario of many adults running for office would radically disrupt the accepted paradigm that says we can only choose from one of two nearly identical parties – both of which are in cahoots with the 1% and both of which resist any change to their privileged position.

In the past, we have consistently returned over 90% of our incumbents to Washington. We have voted for them, again and again, because we were clueless enablers in denial and didn't think we had any other option. But things have changed. Technology, the Internet, Facebook, iPhones, and free and instant communication have tossed the game up into the air.

We return almost 100% of them to office but don't trust 90% of them! Huh?

In the 1960s, I was involved in the Civil Rights Movement. Many of us then felt called to go to the streets. I spent a night in the Okemos County Jail when a bunch of us were arrested for blocking the town's fire station in protest of a housing ordinance in East Lansing, Michigan that prohibited homeowners from selling their homes to African Americans.

I believe we are again in a time of deep discontent and unrest, hearing cries for fundamental change. But now we have an advantage. We can communicate our distress to our fellow Americans much more rapidly than we could fifty years ago. The Internet has allowed things to "go viral." Today, anyone can post a video on YouTube and millions of people can watch it, in minutes. Today, someone can Twitter and a flash mob suddenly appears. Today, we live in a world where 700 million folks commune on Facebook. Today, we have a new ball game. I challenge *you* to dream big and run for office.

And, have fun doing it!

What have we got to lose? Let's *occupy the elections!*

One of the most insidious forms of denial about our political system is the idea that it's "hopeless" and that "one lone congressperson can't make a difference." This is insidious, because if you think this way, you won't vote for a lone candidate, nor will you run yourself. But there are countless examples of a lone congressperson making a difference. Here are some:

John Quincy Adams is the most famous. After Adams failed to win re-election as president in 1828, he served for 17 years as a Congressman (from 1830 until his death in 1848). Early in the 1830s, he began petitioning for anti-slavery measures, and continued persistently, and solitarily, for years. At every opportunity, he sought debate with his opponents and gave speeches on the floor. His actions supported the burgeoning abolition movement. (See The United States Capitol Historical Society – http://uschscapitolhistory.uschs.org/articles/uschs_articles-01.htm)

Senator Robert Byrd in the Senate was also a lone voice, this time in opposition to the Iraq War in 2003.

The point is that having a voice in Congress means that issues can be brought up and discussion about them will be noted in the congressional record. And often, in close contests, one vote can make a difference, and suddenly, the person who cast the swaying vote has influence.

If I were a United States Representative, I would want to tell the truth. I'd like to have the floor and say the following:

> "Ladies and gentlemen, I am honored to be here to serve the American public and this great institution. I would like to respectfully submit the following:
>
> "This body, Congress, the House of Representatives and the Senate, have acted like clowns. We have spectacularly failed the American people. Plain and simple. We have lied to them; we have unethically accepted money from those we regulate in exchange for special favors that have not been in America's best interests. And we have been mean and nasty to each other. We have not been nice people.
>
> "I say to you that I believe it is imperative that we all sign The Money Out of Politics Pledge – every Representative and Senator sitting today in Congress. We must commit to no longer accepting money from corporations, specials interests, Wall Street, or others who expect favors for the cash. We must only accept $100 or less, and only from individuals.

"We must stand up and take personal responsibility for the corrupt political system we have created. If there are those among you who choose not to carry out this pledge, I ask you to please resign. You embarrass all of us with your cowardice, your lack of vision for America, and your failure to be part of the solution to the crises our country faces.

"We must stop the partisan bickering and whining. We must grow up. We must be honest, and we must fix America's big problems. We must sit down together and be the grown-up leaders we were elected to be. We need to make important changes, and we need to make them now. I'm a big fan of Steve Jobs. He would assign a task and be told that it would take, perhaps, 'six months.' " His response would be, 'Do it in four days.'

"This body is responsible for facing and fixing big problems. This body has lied to the American public for decades. It is time to get to work. We must make bold changes. They will not be perfect, and others will refine what we create. In the words of Goethe: 'Whatever you can do, or dream you can, begin it. Boldness has genius, power, and magic in it.'

"We must get money out of politics with a constitutional amendment and public financing. We must end the War on Drugs, which in reality, is a war on America. We must rapidly go post-carbon and invest in sustainable energy. And we must, above all, serve the children.

"Let us roll up our sleeves and create a roadmap for the above, in 30 days."

America has a lot to gain by having new candidates disrupt a frozen system. A system that can't even balance its budget! A system that poisons our kids, fouls our biosphere, and makes us anxious and scared.

You may be concerned that running for election, and serving, costs a lot of money. It does, especially when you are buying glitzy TV, radio, and newspaper ads to frighten the voters or smear your opponent. But the beauty of running a campaign in the 21st century is that the Internet, YouTube, Facebook, and Twitter allow free and rapid dissemination of any politician's platform and promises. I believe that an effective, low-cost campaign can be engineered using modern technology. And I believe that contributions of $100 or less by individual supporters are adequate to cover the cost of running for office.

If enough of us run, some of us will be elected. While we may be few, we will have "broken the spell" of the Establishment's headlock on the voters. Let those who are discontent use the principles of our democracy, our Constitution, and our laws to run for office in a peaceful and orderly way. Let's restore sanity to America.

Go for it! What do you have to lose?

Seriously, call your local city hall or county offices and talk to the elections folks.

Every electoral district is unique in some ways, but their common purpose is to serve democracy. The staffs in county election offices register voters and help prospective candidates file the forms to get on the ballot. When I wanted to investigate running for office, these are the people I went to for information.

The man I talked to in Marin County (just north of San Francisco) was a great civil servant. He gave me the scoop on how to run for the U.S. Congress. He told me to contact all the counties in my district, and to look at the website for the Secretary of State.

The Federal Government's requirements for candidates are spelled out online at www.fec.gov.

There are handy guides and brochures available at the federal site online: a Candidate Registration Toolkit that contains many of the necessary registration and financial forms you need to file; a Campaign Registration Brochure; a 196-page Campaign Guide for Congressional Candidates, with an additional PowerPoint Campaign Registration Presentation, outlining the laws that apply to candidates; a complete guide from the House Committee on Standards of Official Conduct, available from the House Committee on Ethics, regarding disclosure of personal finances; information and forms for reporting campaign finances.

It is true that the process of becoming a candidate is in some ways arcane, and deliberately so. It's a great way for the existing parties to retain power, by making it difficult for individuals to run on their own. There are county requirements, state requirements, and federal requirements. Tedious, yes. Insurmountable, no. I have had an aversion to government bureaucracies, tending to avoid them at all costs and choosing to hire an accountant or lawyer as needed. However, the candidacy process doesn't seem to be that big of a deal. Certainly it's not a big deal if one wants to become a Congressperson, Senator, or President.

Getting on the ballot means staying on task and minding the details. A small price to pay for the opportunity to change the country.

Over 60% of Americans are in sympathy with the Occupy Movement. If a number of Occupy folks run for office, they will make news. Even if it is too late to get on the ballot, it is possible to get the media's attention and, in many elections, to win as a "write-in" candidate.

PART TWO

Now that you've decided to run for office, you will need a platform — a set of principles that you endorse. In the following chapters, I present my take on what I believe are the crucial issues we face in our country today. Please feel free to appropriate any of these for your own campaign, or use them as a launching pad to come up with entirely different ideas.

4

REAL REPUBLICANS AND REAL DEMOCRATS

We have a great system. America got it right, over two hundred years ago. A sane, Democratic government, elected by sane voters, is the ultimate political system. Our institutions are sound. Our Constitution has worked well. The two-party system seems, by and large, to be a good arrangement. We are a proud, strong, and brave country. But we are human and we have our faults. Over the years, we have endorsed some ignorant practices, including terrorizing and enslaving the original Americans, and denying women equal rights. But we have changed. We have made progress in some areas, and we have seriously messed things up in others. And now, it's time for another change.

Numerous recent events have turned the world upside down, and technology has turned on the lights and the microphones. We all can see that the Emperor has no clothes on. He is naked. What I mean by that is this: We see that nearly all of our elected officials in Washington meet the criteria for addiction. They have lost their moral compass. They have become dishonest, immoral, and unethical. We cannot say that they are sane. Many of them went to Washington as good people, but the political system in Washington is corrupt. In order to stay in office, elected officials have had to raise huge amounts of money to buy expensive ads and finance their re-election campaigns. To get money, they have sold out to special interests, corporations, Wall Street, and the hyper-wealthy. They have given tax breaks and regulation favors to these special-interest groups, who have turned around and given the elected officials the money to run their re-election campaigns.

The whole system is now too rotten to try to fix from within. Listening to them "debate" makes me want to clean my garage. Our political debates remind me of the conversations heard at 2 a.m. in any local bar. Our leaders are debating while the Titanic is about to go down. We simply need to say "enough" and pick another group of leaders to try to fix this. The local PTA, fire department, or supermarket employees would do better!

Seriously, don't you agree? I may sound outraged, and I am.

I remember a wonderful ad I saw on TV several years ago. In the ad, firemen are running Congress. They are all in their chairs, wearing their fire-fighting gear. An old, gruff, Irish Captain stands at the podium and asks in a loud voice, "Who wants clean water?" The 435 firemen loudly and in unison say, "Aye." The Captain says, "Opposed?" There is silence. He waits a moment and pounds the gavel down. "Passed. What's next?" End of ad.

We all know we have a water problem. We simply need to come together and fix it.

These nitwits in Washington hire tens of thousands of bureaucrats to come up with the same answer that you, I, and a bunch of firemen *already know*! Then, they form a clutch of committees to discuss the *merits* of clean water, and then, these elected officials go behind closed doors, ignore the scientists, and do what Big Business tells them to do (keep dumping pollutants into the water to protect "economic growth").

But 20% of us do see this and are sickened. *We* need to get past our anger, and that means that we need to act. We need to stand up, like aggrieved people around the world have always done. And done very effectively, as we've seen recently. We must be ready to stand up and serve our country, like honorable Americans have done throughout our history. We must be ready to run for President, Senator, and Representative. And we need to do the same at our state and local government levels.

And we won't need "them," the moneyed interests, to fund our elections. We need to trust this. We now have Facebook, Twitter, and 24-hour news cycles. We have websites like www.opensecrets.org, that tell us who has bought off federal candidates with big campaign donations. If we all run for office, we need to trust that the best of us will rise to the top.

I know. Some of you may be thinking, "What about so-and-so? I like him or her." No. I believe we need to "restart," and begin with a clean slate. If your favorite politician is really good, it will be clear. But think about this. Right now, today, government-sanctioned, coal-burning plants are spewing tons of mercury into our environment. Today! Has your favorite politician been *screaming and yelling* and frantically telling everyone who would listen about this murderous practice? I'm not hearing him or her.

Some of my Democratic friends, and some of my Republican friends, are upset at me, because I tell them that their favorite candidates are accepting bribes from special lobbies. Both parties actively support the removal of Pennsylvania mountaintops to mine coal that heats the environment and puts mercury and CO_2 into the ecosystem. They do this so that they can get money from the coal miners' union and from the mine owners. Some Democrats immorally and unethically accept money from the teachers' union, money that protects bad teachers. The Democrats write regulations favoring Big Law, to get kickbacks. Democrats put their hands out, take millions of dollars from Big Oil, and overheat the planet. The Republicans do the same, but their funding is skewed toward Big Business. None of this is news. These facts have been in our papers and on the evening news for years.

Only those in denial could know the above and think it is "OK." It's not. The highly respected U.S. Attorney, Patrick Fitzgerald, said the following, "You either speak up and do something about it, or you are part of the problem. That's the only way to look at it." That's why we need to see the truth *and* become ready to stand up and take action. As an Interventionist, I know the entire dysfunctional system must change in order to create the space for a new paradigm to emerge. It won't work, it only slows things down, to keep "some of the old" and try to meld it into something new.

No. The 1% – the politicians, the Establishment Democrats and Republicans, those who accept cash from corporations, lobbies, PACs, Super PACs, etc., are the reason that we have this mess. We need to keep it simple and pledge in our campaigns to accept only $100 from anyone, and only from individual people. Keep it simple. This is our country, not theirs. They had their chance and *this* is what they have given us. It is time for the 99% of American citizens not in office to take part in running this country.

As part of this new paradigm, let's rethink the nature of our political parties. I've gone to the Republican and Democratic Party websites, trying to find out what they stand for. Take a look yourself. What's there is a bunch of gobbledygook. I know what I think they stand for. But I don't think *they* know what they stand for!

I believe that Republicans stand for personal responsibility and self-reliance. They uphold the integrity and honor of the individual man or woman, who is strong and independent and responsible. The Republican Party endorses the ideals of self-sufficiency and local government. They believe that every able-bodied man and woman must pull their load, no freeloaders. And they uphold the American values of standing up for our country, and even putting their lives on the line to protect these values and our country.

I believe that the Democrats stand for taking care of those in need, the elderly, the disadvantaged, and the children. They sanction using a central government to protect the little guy and to ensure that business does not hurt people. They see the value of the larger community and the role of government as supporting the development of every single individual. They see the larger community's role in making sure that everyone has access to healthcare, safe working conditions, and education. And they uphold the American values of standing up for our country, and even putting their lives on the line to protect these values and our country.

Which group do you identify with? If you had to pick one right now, which would you choose? Do you lean to the right or left? I have to admit that this is a test. I'll let you in on my agenda in a minute.

But which party did you pick? You may think of yourself as an Independent, but I'll bet you did lean toward one of the two parties above. So, if you had to choose, which one would it be?

OK. Now I'm going to put on my Family Therapist hat and give you a lesson in mental health and what makes good families.

When it comes to relationships, every one of us has two goals. And these goals are in conflict with each other. The first is that each of us needs to take responsibility for ourselves. If we are adults, no one can or should take care of us. The second is that each of us must "work things out" with those we are in relationship with: our parents, spouse, children, neighbors, fellow workers, and countrymen. In other words, to work things out with each other. Family therapists call this "the differentiation of self, while in relationship." It turns out that there is no limit to our personal power, personal agency, and autonomy. And there is also no limit to how close, loving, and emotionally available we can be with another person. If we are in an emotionally close relationship, we have to deal with endless conflicts, because each person is different. Balancing these conflicting needs is the challenge that every person faces, every day. People in healthy relationships will always find a way to work things out and have fun.

A good example of this happens in families with teenagers. Children need parents who will guide them and keep them safe, and who will set boundaries and say "no" when it is appropriate. Upon entering adolescence, a child naturally begins to become more independent. The teen's drive for independence often conflicts with the parents' need to keep their teen safe. We want teens to stand up for themselves and to strive for freedom. And we want loving parents to say "no" when they feel the teen is getting too out-of-bounds. This process naturally leads to conflict. But in a healthy family, the conflicts get worked out and the teen learns both about boundaries and independence.

We want families who will support the individual development of each of their members (the Republican in each of us, that leads to self-reliance). And we want families who will support emotionally close and intimate family relationships (the Democrat in each of us, striving for cohesion and intimacy with one another).

Are you getting it? The core values of both the Republicans and the Democrats are right. Re-read the paragraphs above that describe the two parties. Both of them are right! They simply advocate different qualities, all of which are generally found in functional families and functional relationships.

Our current leaders are not functioning on behalf of the American family. Their dysfunction is glaring and obvious. The fact that they are putting each other down, instead of working things out, is a big clue to their dysfunction. As a family therapist, I often ask myself the following question: "For a person of what age would this behavior make sense?" What do you think? To me, it seems that our leaders are behaving more like teenage jocks competing to "win" than grown-up adults, calmly sitting down and working together to solve the problems at hand.

One of the reasons our leaders have strayed so far from healthy relationship behaviors is that the 1% who possess the money, property, and power have wielded a disproportionate influence over the population. They have behaved like out-of-touch parents whose focus has strayed from taking care of the family. The 1% in power have influenced our democratic governments since we started, even though our founding fathers offered a process that, in theory, gives the power to the people. The problem is that ongoing corruption has resulted in a failure to reach the ideal envisioned by the founding fathers – an America that functions like a healthy family.

But something has changed recently. I believe that a combination of America's psychosocial development, the technological revolution, and factors that I don't understand, have brought us to a "tipping point." I believe that America is ready for a new start that will lead us to a much saner democracy, one that operates like a functional family system.

Of course we all support self-reliance and autonomy, and of course we all want intimacy, connection, and emotional availability. Who could be against any of these things? Healthy people embody aspects of both parties. We need to support the core goals of both the Republicans and the Democrats.

We can no longer support the current politicians who masquerade as "Republicans" and "Democrats." They forgot who they were and what they stood for when they got all mixed up with the fat cats, backroom deals, and lobbyists. The 1% have lost their way.

We all need to support Republicans, as the guardians of individual rights and the sentinels who will support and encourage personal development. There are a lot of individuals who understand this and who would be much better Republicans than those who are currently serving. Almost any good teacher or family therapist would be a "good enough" Republican leader. These folks naturally support the personal growth and self-sufficiency of the individual.

And we really do need to reduce Washington's role in our lives. Our government has become like a giant octopus that sucks money from us. The first President Bush gave a great analogy for what the problem is with how the federal government works. The following is the example he used:

> *Most of us have water heaters that heat our shower water. We go to the shower, turn the faucet, wait a minute; hot water comes out. That's an example of local government. Now imagine that the knobs for the hot*

water were on a water heater located two floors below, in the basement. We would go to the basement to turn the knob. Climb the stairs and see if the water is the right temperature. If the water were too hot or cold, we'd need to go back to the basement and adjust the faucet, perhaps multiple times. And then when we were done, we would need to go back to the basement again to turn off the water.

This, said the senior President Bush, is how the federal government fails at managing things that should be done at the local level.

We need to move more of the federal government's services to the local level. We all could be more Republican, more self-sufficient, and more adult. We need to see that "Big Daddy Washington" is not the answer. Sorry. This means that many of us will need to grow up and become more adult. There should *never* be politicians or a lobby that supports those who play victim (and there are millions of Americans who currently are playing the role of "victim"). Everyone needs to stand up and pitch in, even if it is only to do volunteer work planting the many millions of trees needed to suck up excess carbon dioxide in our atmosphere.

And if a business is acting irresponsibly, we will need the Democratic part of us (that says "we are all family") to come in and lay down the law and set firm limits. There are many thousands of businesses that pollute the environment. Some examples of us engaging our Democratic side include: the Clean Water and Clean Air initiatives; or the laws that protect us from lead in paint, or asbestos in insulation. We want a vibrant, free market that allows for innovation and supports business, but we want the common welfare to be protected, also.

We need to support the Democrats as guardians of the general welfare. We need to support that healthy aspect in all of us that wants to protect the family, in this case, the American family. We need to see that our children get adequate education and healthcare. Almost any healthy grandmother would make a much better President, Senator, or Congressperson than the dysfunctional leaders we currently have in office.

We need both of these parties, working together for the best outcome.

But instead of being our humble servants and serving America, our current leaders are driven more by greed than morality. They are obsessively and compulsively lying, cheating, and stealing from us. Right now, they are acting like the out-of-control kids in the book *Lord of the Flies*. It is truly embarrassing to watch, which is why many educated citizens are too frustrated to even get angry. It really is that insane.

Would you invest a few hours a month to restore our country to sanity? You can voice your opinion, or support a sane candidate's campaign. Or imagine running for office! Yes, *you* for President! Yes, *you* for Senator or Representative. Imagine if everyone showed up and brought sanity back to Washington and local government. Imagine everyone standing up for America!

We can do this. We can take back our country.

I'll prove it to you. Something like this has already happened many times in the history of the world. The Velvet Revolution occurred when millions went to the streets and overthrew the communist government in Czechoslovakia in 1989. The Orange Revolution occurred when people went to the streets in 2004 and forced a corrupt government in Ukraine to re-do a rigged election. Gandhi led millions in non-violent protests that led to India's independence in 1948. Martin Luther King, Jr., inspired by Gandhi's non-violent approach to public demonstration, led America to sweeping changes in our laws, and a public recognition of our institutional racism.

In October 2010, my wife and I, and 200,000 others, went to the Washington D.C. *Rally to Restore Sanity*. That event, along with what has happened in the Middle East, was an inspiration for the creation of my first book, *Intervention on America*, as well as for this book. This gathering, organized by comedians Jon Stewart and Stephen Colbert, was dedicated to countering the craziness and insanity that we all see. It called on us to renew rational conversation at a national level. Two hundred thousand people showed up on the National Mall, with banners and cameras, and peacefully sang, and laughed, and talked, and listened to bands and to speeches by both Stewart and Colbert. And, we *had fun*. Americans like to have fun. We are a joyful and loving group of folks.

We need to do it again. And we need to tell our friends to show up. Tell your friends you want them to run for office. I'm not kidding. We can do this thing. We have reached the tipping point. It is happening all around the world. The news is coming faster and faster. We are getting linked up, more and more, with one another and with the world.

We need to have honorable Republicans in office who understand their task and are ready to serve our country. We need to have honorable Democrats in office who understand their task and are ready to serve our country. And we need to get off the fence! We are all for healthy families, and we are all for strong, healthy individuals. I suggest, to really and fully comprehend this, that you switch parties. Try it. It *really* doesn't matter!

Seriously, if the core values of both parties were to represent the two different aspects of a healthy person, a healthy relationship, and a healthy family, then why would you not support both of them? We need to get rid of our pathogenic beliefs from the old paradigm. We need to toss them aside and allow the possibility of a very different political system, in which both parties disagree and struggle with each other as they press their agenda. But at the end of every day, they embrace each other and laugh, because they see the other party is also right and very necessary.

Take a moment. If you can't really imagine yourself in the other party, seeing the rationale of both, you are not getting the full picture of this paradigm shift. You may still be identifying with your party and rationalizing your affiliation in order to "push your agenda."

Perhaps it would be helpful to imagine re-naming the parties. The Democrats could become the "Family Party," and the Republicans could become the "Personal Responsibility Party." All serious adults would support both parties' goals. In a few election cycles, we could actually re-name our political parties to reflect new democratic and political realities that are based on sound mental health practices.

Each of us must grow up and take responsibility, and wisely support healthy Democrats fulfilling their mandate, and healthy Republicans fulfilling theirs.

It's time for a change!

And it is time to start thinking about the wisest among us whom we would love to see as our next elected officials. Seriously. Do this. Dream big. Our next leaders are folks that are not currently on the political stage. We may not even know who they are, and for sure, we have not imagined them as political leaders.

Until now.

Here is one example of a popular man that no one has ever considered as a political figure. He is an American citizen and was recently on the cover of China's edition of *Newsweek*. He was described as China's "most influential foreign figure." He is like a rock star in Asia. People scalp tickets to see him in Japan, South Korea, and China. 15,000 Harvard students have taken his class on "Justice." Can you imagine this brilliant and popular man as the President of the United States? His name is Michael J. Sandel. This man and many thousands of other principled and smart Americans would be wonderful, inspirational, and honorable leaders.

In this new paradigm, I believe we each need to grow up and take responsibility: for our lives, for the children of the future, and for our planet.

I have an amazing life in Northern California. I have a wonderful wife, nice home, great friends, and a rewarding and meaningful job. But I don't think I have a choice to stay the same. I don't think any rational, sentient human who understands the reality of our nation's predicament and the plight of its citizens has the option to stand by any longer and do nothing. It's that bad. We must all act. This is just like the crisis in the world that led to World War II, only worse. This problem is more pervasive, and closer to home. Back then, everyone needed to step up and pull together. They rationed gas and sugar and butter, and everyone understood why they were doing this. We are on the Titanic, and, like those steering Titanic, our government's incompetence and corruption, our country's social inequity and neglected children, and the worldwide environmental degradation, are steering us into an iceberg. Our current path is not sustainable. We've got to get together and create change.

A lot of wise people agree with me. A recent poll said that 90% of Americans were unhappy with Congress.

The truck driver in Cleveland, the paralegal in Atlanta, the elementary school teacher in Dallas, the insurance salesman in Tucson, the camp director in Wisconsin, you, I, and others can do this thing. We can storm the cockpit of this hijacked country. We can all say, "Let's roll."

Our country is in dire need of radical change. Let's look, one by one, at the areas where we must take sensible measures so our nation can survive.

The following chapters are statements on "what I would do if I were President." In 2012, I won't be running for President, I'll be running for U.S. Congress from California's 2nd Congressional

District, where I live. But here I'm modeling what it would look like for *you* to run for President of the United States. I'm doing this to model for *all of us* what I feel we all need to actually do. I believe that each of us must seriously consider standing up for America and serving, in order to manifest this new political paradigm. And I hope this book moves millions to do what I am doing. We all need to rise up and take our country back from the misguided people and the dysfunctional systems that have brought us to the precipice. We need to "occupy" the election process. We need to see that the current parties have become part of the 1%. We are the 99%. We have the numbers to actually use the democratic process to replace the Establishment Democrats and the Establishment Republicans with new Democrats and Republicans who are grown up and who can simply use their common sense to tackle America's big problems. I'm hoping that you all run, or that you find honorable men and women who will run, and replace the 537 leaders who are currently in office.

You can count on *my* vote!

5

GUIDING PRINCIPLES

What distinguishes human beings from other animals is their larger and more developed cerebral cortex. The human brain is capable of amazing feats, both good and bad. On one hand is the brilliance of Beethoven, Michelangelo, and the folks who got us to the moon. On the other hand is the work of Hitler, the KKK, terrorism, and poor environmental choices that are destroying our planet. Some of us use our minds to create wonder and joy and harmony; and some of use our minds to create division, pain, and suffering.

This dichotomy is reflected in the behavior of our nearest evolutional relatives, the Chimpanzee and the Bonobo. Bonobos are matriarchal and live in peace. Baby Bonobos can completely depend on their elders to protect them and provide them with a safe and sane environment to grow up in. It is as if this species has positive guiding principals that inform its actions. The Chimpanzee, on the other hand, is patriarchal and will murder and rape its own kind. Baby Chimpanzees live in a world that is not safe or sane. We see this "Chimpanzee-like behavior" in human societies all around us. Babies born in Israel and Palestine, for example, are subjected to ongoing terror. The people in these nations, mostly men, seem to be driven by ego and have failed to grasp simple and sane principles, and act in ways that are similar to the Chimpanzees.

The children in these countries would be much better off if their parents switched to a new paradigm, one that resembles a Bonobo-like society where the leaders are guided by more nurturing principles and safety of children is the highest priority.

There are many examples of large social groups that are guided by sane and healthy principles, instead of being led by individuals with personal agendas.

When we have principles that are sane, principles that we place ahead of our ego's need for control, we have the opportunity to provide safety for our children. I believe providing safety for our children needs to be our bottom line. If our behavior puts children at risk, then, I believe, we are behaving like the Chimpanzee. America's mostly patriarchal leaders lack healthy principles. They have put our planet, and all of us, in dire jeopardy. This is why it is imperative that those who comprise the sane middle of America – not the extremists on the right or left – get off their duffs, stand up for sanity, and replace every elected official who cannot embrace the following principles.

I propose the following general principles to guide Americans and America's new, sane leaders:

- Elected officials agree neither to accept any campaign donation from any business, corporation, PAC, or any entity other than a person, nor to accept any contribution of over $100 from any individual.

- Each of us puts the welfare of children ahead of everything. Every government regulation is based on protecting the welfare of children and of future generations.

- Each of us does what we can to protect children from negative influences, including drugs, violence, exposure to upsetting images, and being raised by neglectful parents.

- Each of us understands that we are temporary stewards of the Earth. Each of us understands that we must labor to keep the planet unharmed for future generations. Providing for the welfare of the planet is the job of each of us, and every physical act by any one of us is undertaken with the planet's welfare foremost.

- Each of us looks around and becomes aware of the damage that has been done to the planet, and each of us actively works to repair the damage. Each of us does our best to have a small and sustainable footprint on the planet.

- Each of us honestly strives to understand and respect the underlying values and strengths of both ends of the political spectrum, the left and the right, and to the best of our ability, to use only positive language in our political statements.

- Each of us seeks to understand how our greed and addictions to alcohol, drugs, spending, hoarding, gambling, electronic screens, sex, food, and power keep us from living a full life and prevent us from serving our children, one another, and the planet.

We need to start this new paradigm by getting the money out of politics. We need fair elections where candidates are not bought by funds from Wall Street and Big Business in exchange for special favors or promised tax breaks. We need elections where the outcome does not depend on a candidate's capacity to finance slanderous campaign ads defaming their opponents. We need governing leaders who will make decisions in Congress based on rational thinking, on choices that support the environment and serve our citizens and our country, not on how much money they will receive from some corporation or PAC. Until we remove money from the electoral process, none of the other principles that I propose stands a chance of succeeding.

6

CAMPAIGN FINANCE AND VOTING

Right now, the game is rigged. The money, the fat cats, the 1% who comprise our oligarchy, have structured our federal election policy so they can stay in power. They use their money and influence to ensure that they control the outcome.

Washington's pervasive corruption is again revealed in Jack Abramoff's frank "tell all" book, *Capitol Punishment: The Hard Truth About Washington Corruption From America's Most Notorious Lobbyist* (WND Books, NY, 2011). Abramoff was a high-powered and connected lobbyist, a wheeler-dealer in Washington's power game for years. He stepped over the line, got arrested, and spent over three years in prison. He paints a picture of a Washington filled with corrupt politicans who have gathered power over the years and who, on golf courses and in back rooms, trade that power for cash and for more power, *and every politician in Washington knows this, knows this dirty, unethical, and corrupt truth.* (But does not have the spine to stand up to it!)

He tells of the hypocrisy of a number of the Senators on the committee that was investigating him for breaking the law: they themselves had unethically received money from him in exchange for favors! He calls out earmarks. Most members of congress routinely run up the federal budget with thousands of these special projects for their home districts – bloating the costs to all taxpayers. But, many of these earmarks *often unethically go to benefit those who contributed to their campaign!*

But we voters play a part in this. We want someone else's bridge de-funded but not ours. Abramoff points out DeToqueville's thought that our Republic was in trouble and doomed once the "voters discover that they can vote themselves largesse from the public treasury." Where are the ethical leaders who will remind the voters that while earmarks for their home district sound good, they burden our whole country and raise everyone's taxes? He suggests that it should be illegal for lobbyists to give *anything* to a politician, a political party, or any other entity related to the work Congress does. He also suggests that politicians leaving office be banned from becoming lobbyists. He suggests that they go home and get a job.

We see the result of this corrupt practice on TV, on the Internet, and in our newspapers. What we see is an elected official, a man or a woman who has been pushed through the sieve of political programmers. These "leaders" have had to sell out so much of themselves to their handlers and those who give them money, that the result is a spokesperson, parroting the oligarchy script.

Recently, in the Iowa Straw Poll, Rand Paul came within a few hundred votes of winning. As recounted on *The Daily Show*, no major media outlet reported this! Rand Paul does not fit into their mold. And if someone does not fit into the oligarchy's mold, then Big Media has a tendency to ignore him or her.

Powerful, wealthy, and influential forces shape the outcome of our elections in ways that we can no longer tolerate. Go to www.opensecrets.org and look at what politicians are spending to get elected.

It never made sense to allow large entities like corporations to bribe officials as they do now. And I don't think it makes any sense to allow these same special interests to finance TV advertisements for one candidate or another. We humans are all "brainwashable." All of us. I see an ad for this or that product and I want to go buy it. We all do this. That is why we have advertising: to promote business. And it works. This is fine. But it is not OK to allow the fat cats to use their money for developing slick ads to brainwash the electorate. This is not about selling a product, but about governance of our country, and about our children's future. This smacks too much of something out of *1984.*

We can change this.

They won't change this. They will fight tooth and nail to keep the whole system rigged to their advantage.

But we can do it. Simply vote only for candidates that don't accept money from businesses.

That was easy. Think about it. It will work.

Next: the Electoral College.

Many states are moving to apportion the Electoral College votes as a percentage of the popular vote. Why this has not been done before has never been effectively explained to me. I understand that a committee, two hundred years ago, thought the Electoral College was a good idea, but it no longer makes sense today.

We have had a number of presidential elections where the candidate who received the fewest votes, won!

It's time to change that.

We all need to come out of denial. We, you and I, are 100% responsible for our current political and environmental reality. Democracies are governments by the people. We each need to envision a sane world and then take action to manifest that – run for office, go to the streets, share our views online, attend political events, vote, etc.

Imagine yourself guiding us out of this mess. The following is what I would do. *What are you willing to do to assure future generations a better world?*

If I were President, I would support two constitutional amendments. The first amendment would abolish the Electoral College and replace it with a popular vote. The second amendment would ban campaign contributions from anyone other than individuals – no contributions from organizations or unions or businesses or corporations would be legal. Additionally, there would be a financial cap on the amount of money a candidate for national office could receive from any person. I propose $100 as the maximum allowed.

Why does it cost so much to run a campaign? The reality is that information flows freely in our new technological world. We all get to see and hear the candidates in speeches and debates on TV and on the Internet, for free. The current system is organized around wealthy interests who end up treating us like idiots with their negative and nasty advertisements. Unfortunately, advertising is brainwashing that works: it obscures the real issues and can make us not want to vote at all!

One more thing. I would want an educated historian present at every cabinet meeting. We need to have some historical perspective to ground all of our proceedings.

7

DRUG POLICY

Our drug policy is not working. I know. I treat addiction. And I have known addiction since birth. My father was an addict, and I became an addict. I have been sober for over three decades. I founded, and direct, an outpatient rehab center that treats teen, young-adult, and adult addicts. I instruct graduate students in treating addiction. I am a Professional Interventionist. This is my field. I live it every day.

As we have seen, endless kickbacks from Big Business to our politicians have led to insanity on many fronts. What's happening with drugs in our country today is one of these fronts.

Here are the consequences of the "head-in-the-sand" drug policy supported by the 1% and their purchased elected officials:

Today, children have easy access to powerful narcotics and designer drugs that did not exist one generation ago. Today, at your local public school, your child can buy these drugs. Today, nicotine addiction, which kills nearly a half a million people every year, is not being talked about because our politicians get kickbacks from Big Nicotine. Today, 90% of active drug addicts are receiving *no* treatment.

Today, countries like Mexico and Afghanistan are falling apart, as narcotics gangs challenge the state for control. It is estimated that 70% of the money supporting the Taliban comes from the sale of heroin to America. We are devastated at the number of Americans killed in Iraq; *during this same period, six times as many deaths have occurred in Mexico, because of our drug policy.*

Today, secondhand smoke kills over 50,000 people a year. Today, we are failing to prevent addiction in children. Today, over half of all prisoners in jails and prisons are there because of crimes involving drugs. Today, millions of untreated addicts rob and kill to get drug money. They kill and molest our kids when they're high. Today, right now, someone is trying to figure out a way to offer your child addictive drugs.

This is what you and I have created. You and I are responsible for electing leaders who help create this. This is our "Drug Policy." This is our Drug War.

How is this working for you? It's what you and I are faced with, today.

This is my field. The insanity of drug availability makes me crazy. Every day I look at children who have been damaged by the drugs that we allow them access to. *They are our children*! It is the job of adults to protect children! We are failing. We need to grow up, get our act together, and protect all children from drug use.

A kilogram of heroin costs $1,000 in Bangkok and $250,000 in New York City. The organized drug dealers have the profit motive, and they have far, far more resources than the drug police. When I worked in San Quentin, it was well known that drugs were readily available there. If we can't keep drugs out of prison, how can we keep them away from those who will sell them to our children?

Law enforcement officials are on the front lines of this "Drug War" every day. They see the insanity of our current approach and favor a sane approach to this issue. The following is from the website for the organization, Law Enforcement Against Prohibition: (http://www.leap.cc)

> We believe that drug prohibition is the true cause of much of the social and personal damage that has historically been attributed to drug use. It is prohibition that makes these drugs so valuable – while giving criminals a monopoly over their supply. Driven by the huge profits from this monopoly, criminal gangs bribe and kill each other, law enforcers, and children. Their trade is unregulated and they are, therefore, beyond our control.

> History has shown that drug prohibition reduces neither use nor abuse. After a rapist is arrested, there are fewer rapes.

After a drug dealer is arrested, however, neither the supply nor the demand for drugs is seriously changed. The arrest merely creates a job opening for an endless stream of drug entrepreneurs who will take huge risks for the sake of the enormous profits created by prohibition. Prohibition costs taxpayers tens of billions of dollars every year, yet 40 years and some 40 million arrests later, drugs are cheaper, more potent and far more widely used than at the beginning of this futile crusade.

We believe that by eliminating prohibition of all drugs for adults and establishing appropriate regulation and standards for distribution and use, law enforcement could focus more on crimes of violence, such as rape, aggravated assault, child abuse and murder, making our communities much safer. We believe that sending parents to prison for non-violent personal drug use destroys families. We believe that in a regulated and controlled environment, drugs will be safer for adult use and less accessible to our children. And we believe that by placing drug abuse in the hands of medical professionals instead of the criminal justice system, we will reduce rates of addiction and overdose deaths.

If I were President, I would implement a two-pronged approach to our drug problem. First, we need to come up with a comprehensive approach that will protect all children from drug use. Nearly every adult addict began his or her addiction as a teenager. And second, we need to legalize drugs. We need to legalize drugs *in combination with* creating a comprehensive, integrated, national plan that protects *every* child from any substance use, educates the public, and provides treatment for addiction.

What I propose is a radical change in our social norms that would lead to a much saner and more compassionate world, as well as to a much lower incidence of addiction. (And *much* lower taxes.) This change will require a society with a broader vision than we currently have, but I believe it is possible to quickly achieve this goal if we put our minds to it.

Let's imagine a world where drugs are legal and taxed. And let's imagine a world where anyone who is affected by addiction receives treatment, because it is approximately 10 times cheaper to provide treatment than to pay for the legal, social, and medical consequences of addiction. Nearly all organized crime would cease, 75% of our prisons could be closed, and we could retire or reassign the drug police. This would save billions of dollars and reduce the social upheaval that's resulted from making substance use illegal. And let's imagine a world where every child grows up with their brains and bodies free of addictive substances. The number of adult addicts would diminish drastically, because teens who have not used drugs by age 18 become addicted, if at all, at a much, much lower rate than those who use drugs before their brains have matured.

Sounds pretty good, yes?

Some people think that legalization of drugs would lead to more drug use. To these uninformed, let me say the following:

> *"Right now, every drug you could ever want is already readily available!* You must be smoking some weird stuff to think that the legalization of drugs would make drugs *more* available! Listen carefully: capitalism works. Drug dealers sell drugs to make money. Any drug-seeking person can land on any part of the Earth and, within hours, if not minutes, find and acquire all the drugs they want. Only those who have never visited 'the street' could possibly believe that the legalization of drugs would make drugs more available."

The problem is that currently, drug dealers sell, and give, drugs to children. Which, from a marketing standpoint, makes a lot of sense. They are creating more customers. Perhaps drug dealers learned this tragic scam from our elected officials and Big Nicotine, when both were actively peddling deadly tobacco to children. (Or, today, doing very little to prevent marketing tobacco to kids.)

Statistics have shown that teens who do not smoke cigarettes before age 18 have a much, much lower lifetime chance of becoming addicted to nicotine. The reason for this is simple – by age 18, their brains have developed enough wisdom to understand the stupidity of inhaling burning leaves. Sane adults see smoking as a really stupid practice, one that leads to addiction and to death. Up until just a few years ago, the tobacco industry, government officials, and we enablers allowed advertising of tobacco to children for exactly this reason: children, and younger teens, do not have the judgment to refrain from smoking. By age 18, young adults are beginning to be able to think enough to not fall for slick advertising or peer pressure.

Research has shown the tragic cost – to children and society – of minors' exposure to drugs.

At what age *should* young adults be allowed to have access to drugs?

Perhaps the question we need to ask is, "when does the brain actually mature, and when have we grown up enough to make good decisions?" Neurological research has shown that the brain continues to grow and develop until around age 25. Would 25 be the best age at which to make drug use legal? To keep it simple, perhaps we start out by stipulating 18 as the age at which to allow legal access to drugs. Then, every two years after that law is in effect, we move the legal age for drug access up by one year, until we reach age 21. In the United States, teens at age 16 are allowed to drive; at 18, they can vote and own rifles. By age 18, teens have developed some level of maturity, although their brains and capacity for judgment are still growing.

Our new drug policy would include the following two laws, which would be interlinked. The first law would mandate that absolutely no child under age 18 would be permitted use of any recreational drug. The second law would state that there would no longer be any laws restricting the right of adults to ingest any substance.

These two laws must go together.

The only way we can have the freedom of legalized drugs for adults is to effectively protect children from drugs and the harm they cause. Children have not yet developed the judgment necessary to make adult decisions, like those involved in driving a car or handling firearms. Children who use drugs are at a disadvantage. The younger a child is when introduced to drugs, the higher the probability they will become addicted, and even if they don't become addicted, the higher the chance they will not "make it." These drug-using teens often become the dysfunctional adults who can't take care of themselves and who burden our social, law enforcement, legal, and healthcare systems.

We also need to take another look at adult drug use and how we, as a nation, codependently enable addiction.

We allow the psychiatric mental disorder called addiction to exist, then give impaired addicts money (welfare, food stamps, workers compensation, medical care) to support their addiction, and *then we get mad at them for not being able to support themselves!*

Should anyone be able to take drugs when they are not yet capable of taking care of themselves? One of the quickest ways to get an adult to enter treatment is to say, "either you go into treatment or I will withdraw all your financial support – no food, no housing, no car, no cell phone, no money, no nothing." We taxpayers are giving billions of dollars to addicts, and to others who are impaired because of drugs. We dole out money through myriad "safety net" programs. I propose that, in order for an individual to receive government money from these programs, they need to be completely drug-free. And if they are addicts, we need to offer them free and comprehensive addiction treatment. We want these people to get off the dole and contribute their fair share. They can't do that if their addiction has made them insane. It may make us crazy to hear about the food-stamp-and-welfare crowd laying around and watching TV while we pay their way. But the much bigger tragedy is that it is you and I who are enabling mentally ill souls to suffer. I believe this tragedy weighs heavily on our nation's conscience.

And when I see an adult drug addict, I usually see a developmental crisis. I see an adult who almost always started using drugs in their teen years. I see a family system where the parent and society enabled this teen's drug use. And now I'm looking at someone who didn't *make it.* They did not make it to adulthood and are not capable of being self-sufficient. Without an intervention, and an often-costly treatment process, these individuals will need their mommy and daddy to take care of them forever. Or we, the taxpayers, will have to take care of them. They will fill our prisons or become our homeless, who suck up huge amounts of our tax money through various social services.

Nearly all mammals protect their young. And we have a comprehensive set of laws to protect children from harm. We don't allow children to be neglected or abused. Child Protective Services, the police, and the courts will intervene as needed. We don't allow children to work in dangerous conditions. Children cannot drive cars or carry guns until they are old enough to have good judgment. It would be easy to add "no drug use" to the list.

It would be easy. We simply need to wake up and get educated about the facts. And then, make a decision.

It is a parent's job to keep their kids safe. Allowing a child to use illegal drugs is neglect – plain and simple. It is just plain wrong for us to allow any child to damage their body and stunt their bio-psycho-social-spiritual development. We as a society are just waking up to the horrific risks of the deadly drugs that were not around a generation ago, the reality that addiction is clearly a brain disease, and that effective treatment is available.

Every day for nearly 20 years, I have worked with families whose children have become addicted to drugs. Typically these children started smoking pot or drinking in around the 8th or 9th grade. Boom. At that point, development slowed down or stopped for many of these children. It is now two, or four, or ten years later, and these families are finally coming to my office with a huge problem. (10-15% of Americans are or will become addicts, and most of them begin using drugs in the 8th or 9th grade.)

When this happens, I take a deep breath and go to work. What I love is the parent who calls me at the first sign of drug or alcohol use. The *first* sign!

It's simple. The parent of a minor child sees a potential problem, and gets help. The child understands that his or her parents are serious and that there will be consequences if they use substances again. These kids will stop. (Unless they are already well into their addiction – in which case we are lucky to have caught it early and can start treating addiction when it is the easiest to treat.)

The teen will be angry. We expect the teen to be angry. Healthy teens will push the envelope. Healthy parents set clear boundaries. (If a teen is angry, it's actually a really good sign. They are having their natural grandiosity and narcissism shaped by reality. Parents who fail to say "no" are neglecting their child by failing to teach their children about limits and how the world actually works.)

So how do we protect a child from drug use? It's simple. Test them. (Some private schools already test all students for nicotine and other drugs.) A saliva sample will show drug use.

We, as a nation, need to ask ourselves these questions: "Do we think that protecting children from drugs is a good idea? Do we believe that protecting children from drugs, like we protect them from other kinds of abuse and danger, is a good idea? Should they be restricted from engaging in certain actions and behaviors?" Every doctor, mental health professional, police person, teacher, cleric, and nearly all healthy parents support keeping children drug-free (alcohol is a drug).

As a nation, we need to take on the challenge of drug addiction in our country. We need leaders who will lead, we need a president who will use his bully pulpit to educate, lecture, and if necessary, to yell, at lazy, incompetent, or addicted parents who fail to protect our nation's future citizens.

There will be a lot of resistance from the 1%, who will lose a lot of money. Some adults will resist keeping drugs from children because they will lose their "using buddies." Seriously! Many addicted parents "turn their children on" to drugs (including alcohol) so they have a companion with whom to get high. There will be resistance from the lawyers, because they make money by resisting things. And, there will be a lot of parents who will need to go to parent education classes and visit family therapists, because they don't yet know how to set boundaries and say "no" to their children.

I believe that a sane population will recognize that parents who allow their children to use drugs are in the same league as parents who abuse or neglect their children.

Some citizens feel that children need the freedom to experiment with drugs. Children have many rights, but the right to harm themselves is not one of them.

I ask you this: can you name one doctor or mental health professional or educator who advocates children having access to drugs (including alcohol)? Not one sane adult wants children to harm themselves. Yes, America would have to change its social norms to accommodate this. But I believe most parents would embrace a process that keeps their children drug-free until they become adults. (Remember, sending kids to work in factories and mines, and beating them, used to be legal.)

If children were protected from using drugs until age 18, how many on their 18th birthday would choose to smoke cigarettes? My guess is that cigarette smoking would almost completely cease to exist as the old addicts die off. (Guess who would go ballistic at this idea? Big Nicotine, Big Advertising and Big Government, all of whom will lose the money they get from the tobacco industry's kickbacks. And I know what happens to an addict when they have their "fix" taken away from them . . .)

In the world that I propose, everyone would be educated about the brain disease of addiction. Addiction would be recognized as a chronic, medical disease, like diabetes, hypertension or asthma, and treatment would be readily available. Parents and children would be educated about the warning signs of addiction. Parents would seek immediate help for their children at the first sign of any use. And this help would be readily available.

What about those who are mentally ill, or homeless, who cannot make wise choices, and who suffer from a wide variety of psychiatric disorders including addiction? What about them? Right now, we spend a fortune on them, and they lie on our streets, suffering terrible lives and cycling endlessly in and out of jails and prisons and hospitals. What about them?

For a small fraction of the money currently being spent on social services, prisons, and lining politicians' pockets, we, as a society, could adopt a compassionate program for mentally ill adults who are unable to care for themselves.

There has to be treatment available that falls between going to expensive mental facilities and living on the streets, or warehousing these souls in cages (jails and prisons). We have come a long way from the lunatic asylums of old, but it is a sad thing how we currently treat our mentally ill.

I wonder a lot about this. Certainly we can do better. There have to be some young idealistic minds out there that can create the next, compassionate program to benefit this population. What we are doing is not kind.

Here is one idea. Could we give the mentally ill a safe place to receive treatment and get well before rejoining society at large? Perhaps facilities could be created on one of the Channel Islands off California or in Puget Sound or off the coast of Maine

This may sound odd, and a million critics will find fault with this idea, but to them I say, "OK, what is *your* plan?" We need only look at the current "policy." These poor souls eat out of dumpsters, sleep in doorways, live in our parks, wander the streets, or are put in cages (jails and prisons) and get no help. Is it better to continue to stand by and deny this tragedy? How long can we ignore these tortured souls among us?

Could we create a society that treats addiction and mental illness humanely and responsibly? We have come a long way as a species, and we can take this next step. It will require leaders with vision. And the impact will be profound. We could eliminate most prisons, reduce taxes, better educate our population, and create healthier families. We could eliminate the specter of untreated addicts and the mentally ill lurking near our children and dying in front of us.

Right now, we are at war with ourselves. Someone said that Osama bin Laden could not have come up with a better plan to disrupt America than our current War on Drugs. It is really a "War on Ourselves." One part of us wants to eat candy, and another part wants a paternalistic government to protect us from ourselves. I believe that we just need to grow up. We can build a society that is honest about drugs. Addiction will come to be seen for what it actually is: a bio-psycho-social-spiritual disease that can easily respond to effective treatment.

Almost everyone has strong feelings on this topic, and we have a lot to think about before we start down the path toward drug legalization.

We might get some insight from anthropologists who have studied different cultures. Humans have historically used a number of drugs in ways that bring communities together. Indigenous cultures throughout history have been using drugs as sacraments; as ways to enhance spirituality and deepen connection to nature. The Native Americans used Peyote, the South Americans used Ayahuasca, other societies have used psilocybin, marijuana, Ibogaine, and, more recently in the west, LSD and MDMA (Ecstasy).

Currently, the federal government is supporting rigorous experiments to confirm what many of us already know. For years, M.A.P.S., the Multidisciplinary Association for Psychedelic Studies, has been quietly promoting legitimate, government-sponsored, scientific research on the positive uses of psychedelics. Researchers are using LSD and psilocybin to treat anxiety in people suffering from terminal diseases. The Pentagon is working with medical doctors to use MDMA (Ecstasy) for treating Post Traumatic Stress Disorder (PTSD) in war veterans. And research is now being done on the use of Ibogaine to treat addiction.

Many people know about the beneficial use of psychedelics. Research in the 1960s showed tremendous promise for using these drugs to alleviate mental distress and enhance well-being. Bill Wilson, one of the founders of AA, had his lifelong depression helped by using LSD. Some people wonder if his "spiritual awakening" may in fact have been caused by the "Belladonna Treatment" he received in 1935. The government's hysteria in the 1960s and 70s brought legitimate inquiry to a close, although active underground research has continued among professionals around the world. Slowly, science is proving the value of these substances for legitimate medical, spiritual, and social purposes.

In America, two organizations are authorized by federal law to allow its members to legally use psychedelics as part of their rituals. One is the Native Americans, who can legally use Peyote. The other is the Uniao do Vegetal; an organization founded in Brazil, that can legally use Hoasca, also known as, Ayahuasca. Ayahuasca is a psychedelic that has been used by the indigenous peoples of South America for centuries.

Anthropologists who have visited these Brazilian communities report that Ayahuasca-using communities are socially much healthier and more developed than the people in nearby communities who have adopted the "Western Life" that embraces alcohol and nicotine use.

A case could be made that we might be better off as a society if we were using drugs that led to a loving connection with each other, and with nature. These drugs would include LSD, psilocybin, mushrooms, Peyote, Ayahuasca, and marijuana. And we might be better off not using drugs that make us unconscious, combative, angry, and sick, such as: alcohol, narcotics, stimulants, and nicotine.

This makes sense to me, a former hippy, who found love, spirituality, and connection through psychedelics, and ultimately despair, sickness, and insanity when I turned to alcohol.

Lastly, our drug war exposes our nation's racism. The following comes from the recent book by Michelle Alexander called *The New Jim Crow: Mass Incarceration in the Age of Colorblindness.*

From the beginning, the War on Drugs had little to do with public concern about drug use or drug-related violence (which the War greatly exacerbated), and everything to do with public concern about race, particularly with the concerns of poor southern whites.

First coined by Nixon in 1971, the so-called "War on Drugs" was part of the Republican Party's Southern Strategy, the use of racially coded "get-tough" language about crime and welfare to appeal to poor and working-class white voters, who were resentful and anxious about gains made by African Americans during the Civil Rights movement.

In 1982, the year President Reagan officially proclaimed his administration's War on Drugs, crack had not yet hit the streets, drug crime was declining, and less than 2% of the American population viewed drugs as the most important issue facing the nation (*The New Jim Crow*, p. 49.) Nevertheless, the Republican Party's focus on drugs, like its stance on welfare, proved politically advantageous. In the decades following the Civil Rights movement, Southerners would join the Republican Party in droves. After Reagan, Democratic and Republican administrations alike would continue to pour vast sums of federal dollars into the War on Drugs for political gain, with devastating social results, particularly for people of color.

Today, the incarceration rate in the United States is six to ten times greater than that of any other industrialized nation, and no other nation incarcerates such a shocking percentage of its ethnic or racial minorities.

"In major American cities wracked by the drug war, as many as 80 percent of African American men now have criminal records and are thus subject to legal discrimination for the rest of their lives," writes Michelle Alexander. "These young men are part of a growing under caste, permanently locked up and locked out of mainstream society."

Research studies have consistently shown that blacks are no more likely than whites to commit drug crimes. In fact, a study published in 2000 by the National Household Survey on Drug Abuse found that of all groups, white youth were the most likely to possess or sell illegal drugs. But while the vast majority of drug users and dealers in the United States are white, three-fourths of people imprisoned for drug offenses are black or Latino.

Federal drug policy and conservative court decisions have given local and federal law enforcement agencies unprecedented leeway in stopping and interrogating possible drug offenders. And there are powerful monetary incentives, in the form of drug forfeiture laws and federal grant programs, to round up as many people as possible. Not surprisingly, drug sweeps are not taking place on white college campuses or in suburban neighborhoods, where illegal drug use is as prevalent as anywhere else, but in poor black neighborhoods. And those most likely to be convicted of felonies are not drug "kingpins," who can afford meaningful legal counsel, but non-violent offenders pressured to plead guilty, whether or not they are guilty. Because of the drug war's harsh sentencing laws, "drug offenders in the United States spend more time under the criminal justice system – in jail or prison, on probation or parole – than drug offenders anywhere else in the world." (*The New Jim Crow*, p. 181) Once released from prison, "they will be discriminated against, legally, for the rest of their lives – denied employment, housing, education, and public benefits." (*The New Jim Crow*, p. 181) This includes the right to vote in most states.

I recommend Douglas Blackmon's *Slavery by Another Name* and Michelle Alexander's *The New Jim Crow: Mass Incarceration in the Age of Colorblindness* for a detailed and comprehensive picture of how the promise of emancipation and Reconstruction in the late 19th century, and the promise of the Civil Rights movement of the mid-20th century, were betrayed first by Jim Crow, and then by mass incarceration with the War on Drugs.

We all need to come out of denial. We, you and I, are 100% responsible for our current political and environmental reality. Democracies are governments by the people. We each need to envision a sane world and then take action to manifest that – run for office, go to the streets, share our views online, attend political events, vote, etc.

Imagine yourself guiding us out of this mess. The following is what I would do. *What are you willing to do to assure future generations a better world?*

If I were President, I would propose forming an advisory group of wise adults whose task would be to accomplish two goals. The first goal would be to come up with a comprehensive plan that would lead to the elimination of all recreational drug use for anyone under age 18. The second goal would be to legalize all drugs.

I would, within 90 days, present this plan to Congress for additional study and implementation. I would hope to sign this bill into law in another 90 days. It need not be perfect, but it would be a serious and necessary start.

I would create a cabinet post, the Secretary of Substance Use. This Secretary would be responsible for implementing the advisory group's recommendations, which would be along the following lines:

1. We protect children's birthright to healthy brain development by prohibiting drug use until age 18.

2. We utilize all resources to see that children are drug-free. We expand the Child-Abuse Laws to protect children from drug use. We educate the public and encourage all parents, doctors, and law enforcement officials to assess all children for drug use.

3. All drugs become legal for adults, aged 18 and over, and are taxed like we currently tax alcohol and tobacco.

4. 100% of the money collected from taxing drugs would be used *only* for education and research about substance use and prevention and treatment of Substance Dependence.

5. We would disseminate the message that allowing any child access to drugs is illegal.

6. Substance Dependence would be recognized as a medical disease, and all individuals suffering from this disease would be treated, for free, using funds from the taxes on these substances.

7. We would inform the public that successful addiction treatment, to be effective, *must include the addict's enablers.* The enablers are those who fail to confront (and therefore passively support) substance use.

8. We would provide treatment for all inmates who suffer from substance-related disorders. We would free any inmates whose only offense was related to substance use, substance possession, or sale of substances.

9. I would propose the following Constitutional Amendment: "All laws prohibiting the sale and use of any and all substances are hereby repealed. Further, the taxes on the sale of these substances shall be used only to protect children from substance use, to treat addiction and codependency, and to educate the public about substance use and treatment."

The drug policy we have now is insane! Seriously nuts.

How did Amsterdam's legalization of heroin use result in almost zero use among the young? Perhaps observing the ragged, woebegone, and elderly heroin addicts lining up each morning for their daily dose was enough to disgust young people and repel them from adopting the habit. It's not "cool" to be like them! As we emerge from our collective denial, we will see the absurdity of our current prohibition laws.

It is not the government's job to parent us!

8

TREATMENT FOR ADDICTION AND CODEPENDENCE

Homo sapiens has come a long way. We got out of the trees and learned to stand up, make fire, herd animals, and farm. We developed the wheel, and made steam engines, and sent a man to the moon. Today, our technology has transformed just about everything. We have technology that allows most cultures and tribes to communicate and share their wonders. One would think that these accomplishments would put mankind in a really good place.

Except for one very big problem. I believe the majority of Americans, to a greater or lesser degree, meet many of the criteria for addiction. I fit into this category. I am a recovering addict with over 30 years of sobriety.

Craving, loss of control, adverse consequences, and chronic use of the substance or behavior for a long time are the markers of addiction. We all understand that alcoholism is an addiction, and many of us understand the recovery process from addiction. But I believe that most of us have difficulty seeing that many of our common behaviors also meet the criteria for addiction, and that we would benefit from learning how to change and become healthier in these areas.

Take compulsive eating, for example. I live in the San Francisco Bay Area, and our culture is healthier than is the culture of some other parts of the country. As I travel outside of the Bay Area, I am amazed at the number of obese families. Whole families have somehow gone insane and burdened themselves, their children, and the rest of us, with higher medical costs. There are rare, medical exceptions that explain this condition, but the vast majority of these families have succumbed to addictive eating. They know they are fat. They know they would be happier if they were healthier. But their behavior is addictive – they crave their food, they can't control it, it is causing adverse consequences, it has been going on for a long time, and it is getting worse. They are addicted.

Here is one way of looking at this. The drug dealer came along and said, "Hey, come over here. I've got something you will really like. Here, try it. It's free!" The dealer, of course, is Big Food, and their drug is some amalgam of sugar, fat, and salt. And it might not be free, but it is cheap. It is cheap because our government and our tax dollars made it cheap by giving 14 billion dollars of our taxes to Big Farm and Big Food to produce it, *below cost*. (And of course, Big Food then bribes the politicians with re-election money in return for that favor.)

Members of these fat families, one in three Americans, are the victims of an addictive system, just like millions of nicotine addicts are the victims of our elected officials colluding with Big Nicotine and pushing their drug on children, in order to feed *their* addiction to money and power. One in three Americans has been exposed to enough chemically altered, flavor-enhanced, nutrition-depleted food – and advertisements for this kind of food – that they have become addicted.

There are many kinds of behavior that can lead to addiction. These range from excessive TV-watching to compulsive eating, ingesting chemicals, spending money, pornography, computer gaming, and the list goes on.

The bottom line is that the times have changed, and that, for the first time in human history, we have some new problems that need our attention. A hundred years ago, most Americans were simply trying to "get by." They needed to work hard to get food on the table and keep the house warm. While many Americans are still just trying to get by, the times have radically changed. Teens today have easy access to drugs. Fast food and Internet porn are ubiquitous, and many teenagers seem to have merged into electronic screens. We need to acknowledge that addiction is a very big problem; that it affects us all. Taxes would go down significantly if we got a handle on this public health crisis. We would not have to pay the medical costs associated with the 45,000,000 nicotine addicts. We would not have to pay the medical costs for the one third of all babies born after the year 2000 who will become diabetic. We could eliminate 70% of the expenses for police and jails and prisons – which house three times as many addicts as criminals – if addiction were seriously reduced.

It is estimated that over 40% of families are impacted by addiction, whether the addict is a parent, child, or spouse. What is the cost for this? The mental health of America is simply the sum total of the mental health of its citizens. Does it not seem odd that nearly half of our population is exposed to the insanity of addiction, and that this problem is not being addressed directly?

The reason addiction is not being talked about is clear. The addict is almost always in denial. If we have leaders who are addicted to money and power, we would expect that they would not be interested in bringing up the subject.

I like David Linden's book: *The Compass of Pleasure: How Our Brains Make Fatty Foods, Orgasm, Exercise, Marijuana, Generosity, Vodka, Learning, and Gambling Feel So Good.* In an interview aired on National Public Radio, he said, in effect, that he wanted to *enjoy all the pleasures of life, but in moderation!* There is nothing wrong with almost any behavior that raises our dopamine level if we can do it in moderation. In fact, I believe that is one of the secrets of a well-lived life. How many healthy ways can we find to increase our dopamine levels? Unfortunately, many of us unknowingly have crossed over the line from pleasure to addiction and could benefit from some guidance on this issue.

But first, America needs to come out of denial. In my book, *Intervention on America*, I show how our leaders are addicted to money and power. We need leaders who are not addicted to lead us in a discussion about addiction and its treatment.

And we also need to challenge the drug-treatment industry to come out of denial. Current research in mental health clearly demonstrates that the unconscious codependent dynamics in family systems often enable and support addiction. However, addiction treatment has not caught up to the research, and nearly all treatment programs fail to offer one-on-one, long-term, professional treatment to these codependents, and this is the primary reason that these programs have such low success rates.

In many ways, addiction is simple to treat. We need to acknowledge our inability to control that which we cannot control, reach out for help, and follow treatment recommendations. With support, nearly all of us can stop our addiction just for today, and if we get support, we can probably do it again tomorrow. As they say, it's "one day at a time."

Typically, however, it is the enabling codependents who are the problem. Although these folks have the best of intentions of helping the addict recover, they actually perpetuate the addiction. If we could ship all the codependents to the moon, many addicts would crash and reach out for help.

We all need to come out of denial. We, you and I, are 100% responsible for our current political and environmental reality. Democracies are governments by the people. We each need to envision a sane world and then take action to manifest that – run for office, go to the streets, share our views online, attend political events, vote, etc.

Imagine yourself guiding us out of this mess. The following is what I would do. *What are you willing to do to assure future generations a better world?*

If I were President, I would appoint a Secretary of Recovery. This individual's mandate would be to bring awareness to the public that addiction is treatable and recovery is possible.

I would ask him or her to look at the addiction research and treatment programs the government has developed. I would bring the treatment of addiction and codependency out of the closet and into the light, where we can see the magnitude of the damage that addiction has done to America, and to the children who grow up in this world.

I would ask medical schools and mental health training facilities to expand their education on addiction and codependence. And I would see that some of the money obtained from taxing the sale of legal drugs goes to pay for public-service advertising, and to educating the public about the disease of addiction and codependence.

I would invite all of us to read Gabor Mate's book, *In the Realm of Hungry Ghosts,* in order to understand that addiction, codependency, and mental illness often stem from stress that children experience in early life, and that we all need to redouble our efforts to provide the optimal environment for families with young children.

And I would open up the White House to 12-Step meetings, and as a recovering person, I would go to these meetings.

It is time for us to understand the nature of addiction and codependency, the value of treatment, and the significance of the recovery process that can allow all of us to be restored to sanity.

9

ENVIRONMENT

This topic is painful. Who hasn't had their heart broken at what is happening to Our Mother Earth? Remember Joni Mitchell's song about how they "paved paradise and put up a parking lot?"

For millions of years, the Earth and Mother Nature have unveiled their wonder. Man evolved and learned how to hunt and gather and live sustainably on this planet. For a million years, man and nature got along. And then, a moment ago in galactic time, we went crazy. We went insane. We figured out how to set carbon on fire, ignored the effects of our actions, and now we're on track to kill Mother Nature and end all life, if we don't turn this around! It may already be too late.

The Native Americans lived in peaceful harmony with the earth. We chose to disregard their sustainable systems, and now we've relegated these people to a few reservations where they subsist on a fraction of the land they used to protect. If we'd left the Native Americans in charge of our natural resources, would we be in this bad a fix?

It looks like Einstein was right – we are going to destroy ourselves. It is that serious.

Nothing demonstrates this better than the way Big Business, and Big Government, in collusion with Big Union, have gone absolutely insane and destroyed large parts of the Earth.

And we are fools for trusting them. *Seriously, we are the fools who put them in charge!*

The ethanol subsidy game is an example. It is a rigged system, enabled by our politicians. The only people who win are the fat cats in Big Business, the politicians, and Big Farm – the large, mainly corn-growing farmers in Midwestern America. Ethanol is touted as an alternative energy to oil, but it takes a nearly a gallon of oil to make a gallon of ethanol!

So this scheme essentially funds Big Oil. And our government colludes with Big Business to brainwash the citizens of Iowa to accept farm subsidies (bribes) to grow corn that's run through Big Oil's money machines, to make ethanol that's added to gasoline. Who wins? The money addicts in Big Business. And the politicians who get bribes to run their endless campaigns. Big Oil and Big Farm, who get subsidies. Farmers don't seem to mind ruining their grandchildren's lands and rivers, or are so squeezed economically that they can't see another choice.

Does not sound sane to me. To you?

Who *loses*? We all do – our taxes are raised to pay for this charade. And, all of us lose as nature is destroyed and pollutants are washed into the rivers and oceans.

The smallish, blue, third planet from the sun, Earth, is heating up. Its inhabitants are running around at a frantic pace, setting all the carbon on fire.

This last year has shown us what the future holds. In July 2011, every single state reported record-high temperatures! Huge floods and tornadoes happened, and torrential rain fell. This is occurring because our now-warmer air holds more moisture. And it is warmer because we, you and I, this year, have pumped 31 billion metric tons of carbon into it – a new record. And we are in a recession. Wait until world economies are humming again.

Earth's rapid warming is setting off alarms on many fronts. The journal, *Nature,* has recently reported some troubling findings. Scientists at the University of Alaska at Fairbanks are reporting that the ice covering the permafrost is melting. Should this ice melt, it will release vast amounts of methane, and catastrophic amounts of carbon dioxide. Jeremy Rifkin, in his latest book, *The Third Industrial Revolution*, says that if this happened, "there is nothing our species could do to prevent a wholesale destruction of our ecosystems and catastrophic extinction of life on the planet."

Barack Obama talked a good game before he was elected. Many of us hoped *he* would save the environment. But he caved.

He sold out. In his State of the Union address he said, "We have enough natural gas to last 100 years." Am I the only one who wondered about my great, great, grandchildren having no natural gas? President Obama has become part of the insanity. He sold out his influence to the special interests by giving them what they wanted, so they will give him money to spend on advertising to get re-elected. It is estimated that President Obama will spend close to *one billion dollars campaigning, in an attempt to brainwash us into voting for him!*

One billion dollars! What did he have to give up to get that money?

President Obama is opening up more land in Wyoming to dig up more coal, to ship east and burn, pumping more carbon into our air, and spreading more mercury on America's children and into America's rivers. He continues to support the removal of mountaintops in the east, to mine coal in a process that destroys ground water and spews more mercury into the atmosphere (ending up in our children's food), and heats up the planet.

Both Big Oil and Big Union support this. And they are opening up more drilling in the Gulf of Mexico and Alaska. I had hoped that President Obama would be *different.* I now see that I was naïve. I didn't fully understand the magnitude of the power wielded by the 1%. I, like most of us, believed in *the American Way.* I was still in denial of the fact that we are governed by an oligarchy that is run by unethical people.

And the Democrats, champions of the little man, champions of big fixes for big problems, stand around with their hands out, knowing that cash will be coming in to support this madness! The Republicans are also standing there with their hands out, waiting for the bribes and their marching orders.

But now, the Internet has given us, the people, the ability to see that the *whole system* is corrupt.

We all need to come out of denial. We, you and I, are 100% responsible for our current political and environmental reality. Democracies are governments by the people. We each need to envision a sane world and then take action to manifest that – run for office, go to the streets, share our views online, attend political events, vote, etc.

Imagine yourself guiding us out of this mess. The following is what I would do. *What are you willing to do to assure future generations a better world?*

If I were President, I would ask everyone concerned about the environment to read Jeremy Rifkin's book, *The Third Industrial Revolution.* This book challenges all of us to think in terms of the paradigm shift that is necessary for tomorrow.

I would suggest that we all need to go into nature and be still. Some of my most spiritual and enlightened moments have come at such times. We all need to get back to our roots.

If I were President, I would ask Hollywood to take this on. Al Gore's, *An Inconvenient Truth,* was ahead of its time. That movie was like a newly recovering member of AA, walking into a bar in 1935, and saying, "You can stop drinking." No one would have understood what his or her message was. Before AA was founded in 1935, alcoholics had no hope, no help, and no treatment. They all died or went insane. Today, alcoholism is a disease that is simple to treat. When Senator Gore brought his message to Congress, everyone glazed over. No one was ready to hear that message. I would make sure that every person on the planet with a screen to view it had access to his documentary. I would appoint Al Gore as my Secretary of the Environment. And I would see that he received the highest honor America can bestow on its citizens.

I would ask Hollywood to tell the tragic tales of our vanishing wildlife. We all need to know that the Chinese today are shooting elephants so that they can make trinkets! I would propose that we pick a day each year and all go to the streets to spotlight such tragedies. I propose we give China a grade on how it has done to protect their wildlife, and if they have faltered, that we boycott their goods for a month. The same with Japan. This last year, Japan officially sanctioned the slaughter of over 700 whales! They can do this because there are no consequences for their actions. Boycotts work! If I were President, I would personally meet the ship returning to Japan with the murdered whales. Children around the world have been trying to save the whales. We must listen to our future leaders.

I would ask each of us to restore our backyards, if we have them, to nature. Make room for the bugs and the birds and the butterflies. And stop misusing the 90% of the planet that we don't inhabit: the oceans, rivers, lakes, jungles, plains, and air. Once we replace carbon-based energy and have a sustainable energy plan, I would suggest we return our rivers to their natural state, by taking down the dams. We need to see if Our Mother will make it. She has been so terribly molested and attacked that she may overheat and die. We all need to pitch in and pray that she lives. We all need to work to restore her. It will mean that each of us will need to make some sacrifices. And we need to see that this is a multi-generational project. It took Mother Earth millions of years to create her master-piece. It will take many generations to repair what our ego-driven, insane generation has done in just a few decades. There is no way that we can adequately make living amends to Mother Nature. Each of us will die with this on our conscience. Anyone who drives a car or air conditions a home or rides in a jet must wake up to the incred-ible damage we are leaving for future generations to deal with.

In order to put this all in perspective, I believe it would be useful for all of us to visualize a distant future population that lives in harmony with Earth, a population that has repaired this small blue ball. This future population will have stopped burning carbon, restored the Amazon rainforests, reclaimed and replanted swathes of denuded land, and removed dams from the rivers. Our descen-dants will use renewable energy and live in harmony with nature. They will "get out of the way" and wildlife will return. Buffalo will again roam the plains, in millions. Those of us who live in nature will be "off the grid," living like the Native Americans did for thou-sands of years in the midst of this Eden.

Today's population is not unlike the two-year-old who has pooped in their pants and is waiting for someone to take care of them.

That's us folks! You and I. We are pooping in our pants!

The sane among us need to put some sane folks in Washington.

If I were President, every three months, I would throw a dart at a map of the country and pick a city to visit to find out what it's doing to close its landfills. We need to recycle *everything!* One hundred percent. Mother Earth is not an ashtray! I would take my press corps and my photographers to each city's landfills, and walk around and let you see what I am looking at.

Let us elect sane Americans who understand this and can help us create a policy to return the planet to its natural temperatures, and our land to "America, the Beautiful." The people who know how to do this exist. We need them creating our environmental policy. We can be a beacon to the world on sane environmental policies. We can, once again, be admired by the world.

As a U.S. Representative, I will introduce a bill in Congress that proposes the following Constitutional Amendment:

> "Congress and the Executive Branch, in all their actions, will strive to recreate a biosphere like the one that existed when this country was founded."

It will take generations to undo the damage we have done to America. We must come out of denial and realize that Eden and Paradise and Mother Nature are wondrous and all around us, and in the blink of an eye, we have gone insane, forgotten nature's gifts, and ruined our "fruited plains." We need to grow up, come out of denial, and see the bigger picture.

We can do this. Europe has many examples of communities that rely almost completely on renewable, non-carbon based energy sources. We can do this, if we have leaders with vision and integrity, whose goal is to heal the planet. We could do this quite easily if we had leaders who could envision helping the planet recover and creating a sustainable planet and a sane future – leaders who would talk directly to the people. Steve Jobs demonstrated the power of visionary leadership. He built Apple and encouraged his team to create products and services that we did not even know were possible. We need environmental leaders similar to Jobs who can imagine a better future and lead the way there.

10

ENERGY

Sustainability. We all need to make this word a part of our daily language. Is this or that practice *sustainable*? Can we keep doing this, or that, for the next 200 years, without any negative impact on our biosphere?

Can we, for instance, continue to increase our oil use? Is this practice sustainable? Can we expect to extract ever more oil from the Earth? Is this practice sustainable? Can we continue to double the Earth's population every 40 years? Our population was two billion in 1920, and it will be fourteen billion in 2100. A seven-fold increase. Is this sustainable? Only a small minority of the world's population uses oil to the degree that America does. When the world has caught up with us, can the Earth suddenly supply five times as much oil as it does now? Is this sustainable? And, if the population doubles again, and if we use ten times as much oil as we are using now, is that sustainable? How will we get ten times that amount of oil out of the Earth? And what will be the impact on the biosphere of burning one hundred times as much oil as we burn now?

This is the Titanic, headed straight for that iceberg! But our leaders don't see a problem. Because if they did, we could depend on them to tell us, right? We elected them to lead, and we can trust them . . . right?

Insanely, politicians today will look us in the eye and tell us that there is no problem. Why? Because they are lying. Because they are pocketing boatloads of cash! (Or they are illiterate. One presidential candidate actually said that he did not believe the Earth was getting warmer!)

From New Jersey's Governor Christie,

> *"I understand you're angry, and I understand you're frustrated, and I understand you feel deceived and betrayed. And the reason you feel all these things is because you have been deceived and you have been betrayed. And for twenty years, governors have come into this room and lied to you. Promised you benefits that they had no way of paying for, making promises they knew they couldn't keep, and just hoping that they wouldn't be the man or women left holding the bag. I understand why you feel angry and betrayed and deceived by those people."*

There is the saying, "Lie to me once, shame on you. Lie to me twice, shame on me." We are all being played for chumps, and we need to grow up and take responsibility for accepting those lies. We need to start over with honest people in office who have taken The Money Out of Politics pledge.

Big Oil, Big Auto, Big Chemistry, Big Farm, Big Union, Big Law, Big Utility, Big Money: the 1% have gone to the backrooms and scratched each other's backs and made deals. And the word "sustainability" is never, ever, uttered. It couldn't be, because none of their practices is sustainable.

This has to stop. We need an energy policy that rewards sustainable practices and penalizes Earth-destroying, unsustainable practices. We need to implement it quickly, and we need to implement it in an orderly way. Again, think of World War II, when we built hundreds of thousands of ships, tanks, planes, jeeps, and trucks *in three years!* And we were done with the war in four. *Those men and women stood up.*

We need to do that now. We need to switch to solar, and wind, and other sustainable energy sources. We needed to have begun that in the 1960s. We put a man on the moon in 1969. We could have ended the practice of burning carbon, but Big Oil was more interested in profit. It must be done, now. We need to think outside the box. We already have a solar car that has traveled 12,500 miles – on sunlight. We have a solar plane that was able to fly continuously for 24 hours, including at night, using solar power alone. We have alternative energy-using transportation available right now! Imagine what the future might hold if we had a "Sputnik Moment," and realized we have to catch up to the rapid energy innovation of other countries.

We have the technology to do this. Do we have the will?

And can we see that the 1%, with their trillions of dollars and their "bought off" politicians, are brainwashing and scaring Americans with their propaganda so they can get even more money and power, yet change nothing?

Again, Jeremy Rifkin's work with the European Union is worth looking at. His plan, laid out in his book, *The Third Industrial Revolution,* has been evaluated by brilliant thinkers in Europe for a number of years, and aspects of his plan are already being implemented in several European countries. This is doable. The question is: "Do we have time to do what's needed before runaway global heating and population growth and economic problems make change untenable?" Rifkin himself says that this project is a big job, but that he has "not seen a Plan B." Clearly, we need to get moving on a comprehensive plan. Below are the concepts that Rifkin and the European Union have developed, and that I believe are the best game in town:

1. Move from reliance on fossil fuel to sustainable and renewable energy.

2. Reconfigure buildings to become individual collectors of energy.

3. Install hydrogen and other technologies to store energy in each of these buildings.

4. Connect all of us in America to an intelligent grid where we can all share energy and store energy.

5. Move our transportation fleet to electricity.

We *know* we have a global warming problem. We *know* we have a CO_2 problem. We simply need to move from thinking, to action.

President Obama sounded like he had a few good ideas at one point, but Washington's rigged corrupt system and the threat of the 1%'s Super PACs made short order of his renewable energy ideas.

We all need to come out of denial. We, you and I, are 100% responsible for our current political and environmental reality. Democracies are governments by the people. We each need to envision a sane world and then take action to manifest that – run for office, go to the streets, share our views online, attend political events, vote, etc.

Imagine yourself guiding us out of this mess. The following is what I would do. *What are you willing to do to assure future generations a better world?*

If I were President, I would ask everyone concerned about energy to read Jeremy Rifkin's book, *The Third Industrial Revolution*. This book challenges all of us to think in terms of the paradigm shift that is needed for tomorrow.

Then I would ask our most skilled and knowledgeable energy scientists and educators to meet, collaborate, and come up with a plan. The current, elected officials have not been able to come up with a plan. We hired them to do things like implement an energy policy. Would you keep an employee who did not do their job? They have not done their job and we must fire them. I once imagined Obama would create a sane energy plan, but he has caved. He has been driven insane too. He is now in the "Drill, baby, drill" camp. He must go, too.

We need to encourage sustainability and discourage non-sustainability. We need to get real about the true costs of, say, burning coal or oil or natural gas. We must rapidly switch to solar and wind and other sustainable energy sources. We need to turn our furnaces down, or off. We need to turn our air-conditioner thermostats up, or off.

I would gather together a new set of thinkers, ones who have been talking about the solution for a long time, such as Jeremy Rifkin. I'd ask them to put together an energy plan in 90 days and present it to Congress. I would expect Congress to give me a bill to sign in another 90 days. It would not be perfect, but it would be a plan, and a serious start.

Currently, we are ripping off the future and ruining our children's planet. How do you explain that to a child? Seriously, go do it. Find a 5- or 10-year-old child and tell them what you have done. Look them in the eye and tell them what their future looks like. We are the stewards of their world. We need to let them know how we are doing our job.

As President, I would do my best. I would ask all the adults to gather their children in front of a TV, and I would say something like this.

"Good evening, children and others watching me right now. I'm speaking here as your President. The adults in this country elected me, and my job is to attempt to make the world a better place for you.

What I have to say is hard, but it needs to be said. It starts out with 'I'm sorry.' We all say, 'I'm sorry' when we make a mistake that hurts someone else. I know you know that. And I'm sure you do the same thing when you make a mistake.

But this is a really big 'I'm sorry.' And it is an apology from all of us adults, including your parents. The apology is to all of you kids.

About 50 years ago, before you were born, we made a big mistake. We really screwed something up bad. We are trying to fix it, but it's pretty bad. We think you are old enough to hear the truth. We became addicted to burning a really big amount of gas and oil and coal. At first it didn't seem like it was a big deal. But we weren't very smart, and we stopped paying attention, and before we knew it, it got out of hand and we were creating some big problems for our planet by burning so much fuel. It turns out that burning gas and oil and coal releases carbon dioxide into the air, and this outflow of carbon dioxide raises the air temperature.

Burning all this gas and oil and coal has heated up our planet, Earth, which has caused the climate to change, and started melting polar ice caps and glaciers. These melting ice fields reflect a lot of the sun's heat back into space. Without these reflectors, the Earth is heating up even more, which is causing the ice caps to melt even faster. This, in turn, is causing the permafrost – the land in arctic areas that used to be permanently frozen – to melt, which releases even more carbon dioxide into the air.

I'd like to say, 'Don't be afraid.' But I need to be honest with you. This could become a very big problem if we don't fix it. And the reality is that we are not going to be able to fix it completely. We totally screwed this one up, and, speaking for all the adults, I'm so sorry for messing up your planet. You have every right to be really angry with us.

The best we can do now is to slow down this planetary destruction. But it will take many generations to get the Earth back to where it was a hundred years ago. Unfortunately, that burden will fall on you and your children.

I am so sorry to have to report this to you. It is unfair to you. We were not very wise, and we are so very, very sorry.

Bu, Americans can be smart, and resourceful, at times. I'm hoping this is one of those times. I'm hoping that your parents and the rest of the adults in this country will get to work on fixing this problem. Fixing this problem will mean all of us will have to make some, or even a lot, of sacrifices. It will probably mean riding your bike more, and walking more.

And I'm going to need your help, because this will soon become your responsibility. I want you to help your parents do whatever needs to be done. Help them understand how they can save energy. We adults have been so addicted to burning carbon that we aren't even aware when we are doing it.

Hopefully, if we all work together, we can fix this problem.

Again, I am so sorry for how we adults, including myself, have damaged your world, and created a problem that you will have to help solve."

Are you ready to tell the truth about the environment to the kids in your life? I have. I regularly make these amends to my grandchildren. And we are all going to have to make sacrifices. Nearly all of us will resist this. We have become dependent on our carbon-burning lifestyle.

We need to get beyond this self-centeredness, and see the bigger picture; where we can see the wonder of a sustainable planet. Once we are able to do that, I believe we will be grateful and gladly accept the sacrifices we must make, because we will finally have sane leadership that has a sane plan. We will gladly drive our cars less often. We will need to walk more and ride bikes more and take more buses and Skype and use teleconferencing.

If we grow up in a country that speaks English, we can pretty much predict that we will end up speaking English. If we grow up in a country that is addicted to burning carbon, we can pretty much predict that it will not be easy to give up our "fix," our dependence on burning carbon.

We are in a race. Can we change before we hit the iceberg? Perhaps we should park our cars, turn off the lights, turn off the furnaces and air conditioners, until we can look our children in the eyes and tell them that we are all doing everything we can to stop destroying their world.

There is a simple solution to our energy problem. Back in the 1960s, we could have started moving toward a sustainable, post-carbon age. Instead, we've been persuaded by the PR of the 1%, the collusion of our elected officials with the massive oil industry, to fall for the magic of the heat that comes from igniting carbon.

"Wow, look at all the energy released when I set carbon on fire!"

Like children, we have set our planet on fire without thinking about the consequences. Our childish practices have built dictatorships in oil-producing nations, caused millions of deaths from countries vying for oil supplies, and led to the horrific specter of a dying planet.

It is time to set the solution in motion. We, you and I, need to sit down and work together to come up with a brief vision statement and a simple energy policy.

My suggestion for such a vision statement is:

'We see an America whose energy needs will be met in 5 years from 50% sustainable sources, in 10 years from 90% sustainable sources, and in 15 years from 99% sustainable sources. Furthermore, we will all work like crazy to restore the growth of carbon-absorbing plants in America and throughout the world."

As a Congressman, I would suggest that all Senators and Representatives be locked in a room until we can come to a consensus on a sane energy policy. And if any of us is unable to join in a consensus because we have been "bought off" by those who funded our elections, I would ask them to step aside or leave office immediately so that the rest of us can get this critical job done.

There is no reason we can't lay out a comprehensive plan in a matter of days.

As a Congressman, I would support a bill in Congress proposing the following Constitutional Amendment:

"Congress and the Executive Branch, in all their actions, will strive to recreate a biosphere like the one that existed when this country was founded."

And I will continue to support the movement that was laid out in my book, *Intervention On America:* that *we,* the 99% of Americans, stand up to the 1%. I suggest that 20% of the American voters (left, right, and center) are not in denial and are sane, and actually see and understand the oligarchy that is destroying America. Wouldn't it be amazing if this 20% of the voters went to the streets the first Saturday of every month and reminded our elected leaders who they work for? If this movement caught on, 40 million Americans would go to the streets every month.

11

WATER

Sustainability. This word needs to be on our lips a lot if we want our children to inherit the planet our parents and grandparents gave us. One hundred years ago, we humans had a much smaller footprint on the planet. We have fouled our lands and waters and we need to fix it.

In the mid-1940s, when I was five, six, and seven, I lived in Palatine, Illinois, a suburb of Chicago. Down the street from where we lived was a "swamp." Actually, it was probably a little piece of nature man had not touched for hundreds of years, or even longer. I often went there and marveled at what I saw. Each spring, I watched tadpoles turn into frogs. There were fish swimming and turtles sunning themselves on logs and rocks. The air was filled with the sounds of birds and insects. Butterflies and bees passed overhead. There were dragonflies and water spiders skipping around.

I felt excited when a neighbor brought home a huge snapping turtle that had lived for decades in our "swamp." But they'd killed it!

Why does man want to kill?

I believe that since the industrial age, we "modern men" have lost our way. We have become more and more isolated from nature, and we have failed to show our children its wonder.

When the Caucasians landed in America, the rivers and plains were alive and well. The Native Americans lived in balance with nature. We white people, and our capitalism, over time, have run amuck and have seriously wounded Mother Nature.

But I want to prove Einstein wrong. I think we can grow up and act like sane adults, people with common sense. I believe in the best in us. I believe we can turn this around. If we can go to the moon, we certainly can stop fouling our water here on Earth!

I live in the San Francisco Bay Area. Here, we screwed up the Bay water by dumping garbage into it to create more land to fit more houses. Who had this crazy idea? You guessed it. It was the fat cats and their buddies in state and local government. They got rich, and we lost the ecology that kept our water clean and the wildlife safe. They looked at the Bay, Mother Nature's complex and amazing and intricate balance of plants and animals, and they saw *money*.

Sane people looked at the Bay and saw a beautiful, flourishing, delicately-balanced ecosystem. These sane people saw that every square inch of the Bay served a function in nature. The tidelands and estuaries were the filters that cleaned the Bay waters while providing a sanctuary for millions of birds and other wildlife. The Bay was home to an abundance of fish and sea mammals. It had been this way for millions of years.

How could we repair this? Actually, in 1961, three East Bay women helped mobilize thousands of concerned citizens in a movement to Save the Bay. This "Bonobo kind of thinking" has restored thousands of acres to nature, and thousands more acres are in the process of restoration. Thanks to the work of this grassroots effort, in the past 50 years there has actually been an *increase* in the size and cleanliness of the Bay. This is a heartwarming and precious movement. We are a long way from total repair. A long way, but people of vision are headed in the right direction. Here in the San Francisco area, we need to be stewards of the Bay. When we visit Our Mother, we need to heed the maxim: "Take only pictures and leave only shadows."

I live in Marin County, a beautiful area, north of San Francisco. The water that goes down my toilet or sink goes into the Bay. Sadly, my water may contain contaminants that end up in our Bay. Water analysis shows that fish caught in the Bay are contaminated with hundreds of compounds ranging from mercury to cancer-causing endocrine-disruptors, and even penicillin, narcotics, and birth control medications. This is wrong! This is pollution and it must be stopped. Each of us must take responsibility for changing this.

Alex Prud'homme's book, *The Ripple Effect*, says the Hudson River contains cancer-causing PCBs, that there is cow manure in well water throughout the western states, and that most of our waterways contain narcotics and synthetic estrogens, and hundreds of other chemicals. How did this happen? It feels like someone should go to jail. Someone should be held accountable for the immoral, unethical, and insane behavior of the companies that have caused this contamination. Clearly you would think that someone should be imprisoned for ruining our water supply. But the reality is that it is all of us who are doing it. We voters are passively allowing these practices to continue, by not being informed, and by not voting for someone who commits to take money out of politics. We have allowed corrupt politicians and Big Industry to run amuck and pee in our drinking water.

Rivers, creeks, and other wetlands all over America are in trouble. The runoff from industrial livestock feed lots is poisoning downstream waters, as well as the aquifers – the underground bodies of water that supply our well water.

Huge corporations are using Mother Nature as a dumpster! Complex and dangerous chemicals today are poured into our aquifers as a result of fracking. Fracking is a new invention of Big Oil to get *more* out of the land. With Chimpanzee-like behavior, oil companies set off large explosions in the delicate skin of our planet and then pump chemicals, under high pressure, to break up the land so they can extract more carbon to sell.

These 1%-people do not even get the madness of their actions!

Aquifers are unseen bodies of underground water. The rain that lands on the earth ultimately finds its way into these natural reservoirs. These precious bodies of water have been here for millions of years and provide the well water that many people drink. Can you imagine anything crazier than pumping poison into this ancient, fresh water body? The Environmental Protection Agency released a report in 2004 that said that fracking poses "little or no threat" to the water supply!

So, some part of the 1% (Big Oil) had other members of the same 1% (government scientists) do a study that said there was little or no threat from fracking. They said this, even as the evening news was showing people setting on fire the methane that was coming out of their tap water spigot!

Another part of this 1% (Congress) is authorizing companies that are pumping this fracking fluid into our aquifers, to disregard the regulations of the Safe Drinking Water Act of 2005. Congress also authorized Big Oil to keep the ingredients in the fracking fluid secret! (Why?) Some of the chemicals that have been pumped into these ancient fresh water bodies from fracking are carcinogenic; others contain chemicals that interrupt normal growth and development in babies. Arsenic, copper, vanadium, and many other toxic substances have also been released into the water as a result of fracking. It will be impossible to fix this. Any attempt will only damage it more. For thousands of years to come, if any of us survive, history books will have a chapter about how Americans, in a brief moment of evolutionary time, went insane and did something that had consequences far worse even than what Hitler did. It is easy to see why Einstein could say that he did not think *Homo sapiens* was smart enough to figure out how to survive.

Big Oil, and President Obama, and your Senator, and your Representative, are not only continuing the fracking process, but also expanding its use! There is no hope of talking to these leaders. There is no chance that a demonstration will deflect this monstrosity. "Raising gas mileage requirements" and "subsidizing electric cars" are matches being lit in a thunderstorm. We need to get money out of politics, and elect new, honorable representatives, and then have a serious conversation about how to fix this.

Ultimately, these poisons find their way into our lakes and oceans. This is happening at an accelerating pace, and no sane individual can ignore it. It's time to stand up. We really don't have a choice.

> We all need to come out of denial. We, you and I, are 100% responsible for our current political and environmental reality. Democracies are governments by the people. We each need to envision a sane world and then take action to manifest that – run for office, go to the streets, share our views online, attend political events, vote, etc.
>
> Imagine yourself guiding us out of this mess. The following is what I would do. *What are you willing to do to assure future generations a better world?*

If I were President, I would develop a water policy that would mandate that each and every one of us help put Nature back together. The answer is simple, but what it requires will not be easy. We can no longer use Nature as our ashtray. If any water is returned to Nature, it must be pure. Pure. Not mostly pure, not almost pure, but pure. Just like it fell from the sky as rain or snow. That needs to be our mandate. It needs to be our goal. We need to "man up" and make it happen.

I would ask for regulations stipulating that no one can release contaminated water into our water supply. The technology to do this is already available. What happens to the water that is recycled on the Space Station or on nuclear submarines? There are a number of ways to purify polluted water. Here is a list of some of these ways: reverse osmosis, carbon filtration, microfiltration, ultrafiltration, ultraviolet oxidation, electrodialysis, and microporous filtration. The gold standard is double distillation. This needs to be our goal. We just can't piss in our nest! We are smarter than that!

I would ask you to run for City Council in the city where you live. I would ask you to gather your voters and figure out a way to put *only water that is 100% pure* back into the environment. I want all of us to stop *100%* of the pollution. Not 99.99%. Even water that is 99.99% pure is not sustainable, if we take a long view. *We must always take the long view. We must always think of our children's world.*

We simply have to value our planet. I don't think we realize the tremendous psychological burden each of us carries as we repress the knowledge of the damage we are leaving to future generations. We spend thousands of dollars every year buying stuff – some of it unnecessary and useless. I don't have a problem with that. I like to buy stuff. But I know that each of us could give up a little bit of our stuff to restore Nature and live sustainably. *And we would feel good about coming together as a country and making this happen.*

After we've elected new Senators and Representatives, I would ask every one of them to go home to their local towns and villages and get ideas for stopping *all water pollution,* and restoring our creeks, rivers, lakes, and oceans. Americans are smart and industrious, and they can tell us how to make this happen.

Ten minutes from where I live, a local community is restoring a precious waterway. Using taxpayer money, local volunteers are digging out a channel in the wetlands at Muir Beach in Marin County. Until white people arrived, this area was a vital wetland habitat that provided a home for thousands of critters, large and small. Coho Salmon swam up the creeks at Muir Beach to spawn each year, as they had for hundreds of thousands of years. In the blink of an eye, we destroyed this gem.

Today, you can see the bulldozers and the dump trucks and the men and women in hard hats, busy undoing the damage we've done. It brings tears to my eyes as I watch them work. I hope I live long enough to see the salmon return. I hope I live long enough to see the Western Pond Turtle come back to the area. I love to pay taxes when I see that my tax dollars are helping to remedy the problems my people have created.

Each local community will have to come up with its own unique answers. And every three months, I want each of us elected officials to go back to our districts and drink the water from our local creeks, river, or lakes. I pledge to do the same thing. *And if the water is dirty, I will let you know how I feel after I drink it.* As leaders we need to *lead.* We need to tell those who elected us what needs to be done to fix the water. But we need to do something else. We need to educate the citizens in our districts. We need to give them critical feedback about how they have fallen for the Big Lie and how they need to be much more involved in the political system. We can certainly understand why so few get involved. The current American political system is painful to watch, so we do our best to ignore it.

Business will squeal, "But this will drive up our costs!"

I would say, "So?"

Come on! We humans are somewhat smart. When nature calls, we don't just crap and piss where we are standing! Only babies do that.

But this *is* what we are doing. We are crapping and pissing where we are standing.

We have plenty of resources to reclaim our waterways and restore sanity to our water use. We just need to wake up to the out-of-control 1%, our oligarchy, that is using Mother Nature as a toilet. They need to be toilet-trained. Actually, they need to be ousted from office, toilet-trained or not.

It's clear that our current practices are unsustainable. Yes, profit is part of capitalism, but we also must be moral, ethical, and spiritual. Acting with integrity will bring each of us something much more precious than money. That "something more" will be the serenity you will experience knowing that you were part of the solution and not part of the problem. In the meantime, "Congress, Big Business, Big Union, Fat Cats, get the hell out of the way so that we can clean up the mess!"

We get to start this work when the new leaders we elect take office on January 3, 2013.

As a Congressman, I would support a bill proposing the following Constitutional Amendment:

> "Congress and the Executive Branch, in all their actions, will strive to recreate a biosphere like the one that existed when this country was founded."

Mother Nature has had things in balance for millions of years. We simply need to realize that the 1%'s greed is destroying the planet. And we need to understand that it is we, you and I, who are responsible for allowing our democracy to be hijacked by the 1%. And it is we, you and I, who need to stand up and vote them out of office.

12

THE ECONOMY

For years, we have been spending money like a drunken sailor. We need to sober up.

The Iraq war is an example. Who starts a war without good reason? Our leaders started two wars and put the expenses on a credit card. The Iraq war cost roughly a trillion dollars. Who paid for it? Our leaders expect their children to pay for it! They are not only greedy, but they are shortsighted.

We have been fools; we have been sweet-talked by greedy politicians. But we are waking up to a game that is as old as mankind: the rich and the privileged rig the system in their favor; the underdogs work for them. Things have always been this way. Nature whittles the species through survival of the fittest — the strong and favored thrive, and the weak and less fortunate get the leftovers. Today, 400 Americans have more wealth than 150 million Americans! These members of the oligarchy got that way because they have skewed the system in their favor.

The Internet has turned this game upside down, and now *the 1% with the power and the money have suddenly lost their advantage.* They are being exposed. The playing field, for the first time in history, is now level. And, we are also realizing that we, the Sane 20%, have a 20-to-1 advantage over those who've held the power! This 1%, these elected officials, Big Business, and the hyper-wealthy, are waking up to the terrifying reality that the lights are on, they are the stark naked Emperor, and that we clearly see their game.

To paraphrase Phil Collins's song, *In the Air Tonight:* "I was there and I saw what you (the 1%) did, so you can wipe off that grin, because we all see that it was a pack of lies."

The question is: what will we do with this advantage? Was Einstein right when he said that humans are too dumb to figure it out, and that we will destroy ourselves? Or, was he wrong?

Wikileaks, Facebook, Twitter, Tahrir Square, texting, and hand-held computer phones have created a new paradigm. We are in a whole new ball game, but most of us don't actually realize it yet. What the overwhelming majority of Americans know is that our current political system is bullshit. The old joke of, "If you see their lips moving, they are lying," is no longer funny, and we are actually not sane if we continue to tolerate the bullshit any longer.

We have the numbers. We can fix this thing. You and I. Yes, federal spending needs to come down, way down. Yes, the fat cats, the 1% who have more wealth than over half of the rest of us, need to give up some of their money. We need more billionaires like Warren Buffet, who understand this. John McCain has so much money he can't keep track of his own property. In the 2008 presidential campaign, reporters asked McCain how many houses he owned; the candidate replied, "I don't know. Maybe six or seven." And he is fighting tooth and nail to make sure none of *his* wealth gets diverted to crumbling schools and breakfast for American children who wake up hungry.

Warren Buffet and Bill Gates have initiated the *Giving Pledge* that encourages the wealthy to give the bulk of their wealth to charity. Many rich Americans are joining this cause: Ted Turner, Michael Bloomberg, Paul Allen, George Lucas, Mark Zuckerberg, and Jon Huntsman are some of the Americans who are showing us what honorable and wealthy Americans can do.

At the Washington D.C. *Rally to Restore Sanity* in October 2010, one sign said, "Paying Taxes Is Patriotic." We all need to pay taxes; it is patriotic and it is right. We each need to pay for our roads and bridges and fire departments. Greece's economy is failing, in part because Greek citizens see their government's corruption, and they, like their leaders, have decided to cheat also – hence, their country is going broke. It is tempting to do the same thing in America, after the latest rip-off by Wall Street and its federal government enablers. Every capable adult must contribute. It is not right, and it is not patriotic, to avoid taxes.

General Electric is a great example of the rigged game that hurts America. A recent article in the *New York Times* nicely lays this out. (http://www.nytimes.com/2011/03/25/business/economy/25tax.html?pagewanted=all). G.E. hired former government officials, and former I.R.S. officials, to optimize the company's income by avoiding paying taxes. They bribed Representative Charlie Rangel, chairman of the Ways and Means Committee. Mr. Rangel gave G.E. special breaks that allowed the company, in 2010, to pay *no taxes on 4.6 billion dollars of income!* And, right on cue, Mr. Rangel got 11 million dollars in *"donations"* for his home district. Americans were ripped off for a billion dollars in tax revenue that could have been spent benefitting many more Americans. This backroom deal between Mr. Rangel and G.E. took care of each of *them* just fine. The only problem was that most Americans were left out of the loop. This is just one example of how our corrupt system works.

Egypt's Hosni Mubarak had billions of dollars one month, and the next month he was in prison. We are not Egypt. Thankfully, we have solid institutions, and we hope those who have ripped us off will repay us, because it is the right thing to do. My hope is that most of the billionaires will become like Bill Gates and Warren Buffett and do the right thing. We all die naked and alone. *On our death bed we realize that the only thing we get to keep is what we have given away.*

I believe in capitalism, big time. The opportunity for the individual to conjure up something new that enriches all of us is a very good thing, and these individuals should be rewarded. The late Steve Jobs is a perfect example. But the greedy crooks in Washington are blowing this one. I am a small businessperson, and I need to tell you that I hate the government's excessive intrusion into my business. I have four, part-time employees, but my taxes are so complex that I need to hire an accountant! We have a bloated government, hindering the free market, and I believe my approach, outlined at the end of this chapter, will go a long way toward fixing this problem.

In recent years, government officials have accepted kickback money from Big Banks. They have let some businesses "have it both ways." Big Banks wanted to be capitalists when they could make the big bucks, but then they turned into sissies and ran to mommy when they lost their money. No business should be too big to fail. Any business that is too big to fail should cut itself into smaller companies and be left to sink or swim in the market. This is a must, in a free economy.

Our financial state, our economy, is based on trust. The collusion between Wall Street and politicians has taken us to the brink. The trillions of dollars corporations have given to Super PACs has brought us to a tipping point. Just three years ago, many people lost their homes and their life savings when the housing market crashed and the banks collapsed. Unemployment is staggering – more than one out of every ten able and competent American adults has no job. We, as a nation of law-abiding citizens, do not want to return to chaos and mayhem. We need our national economy to get healthy. Right now, the median American has a net worth of about 200K and debt of 50K. We each own $50,000 of the national debt. We need to get our financial house in order. Each of us, including Uncle Sam, needs to have zero debt and a prudent reserve.

Americans are capable of greatness. Are we ready to take the next step?

We all need to come out of denial. We, you and I, are 100% responsible for our current political and environmental reality. Democracies are governments by the people. We each need to envision a sane world and then take action to manifest that – run for office, go to the streets, share our views online, attend political events, vote, etc.

Imagine yourself guiding us out of this mess. The following is what I would do. *What are you willing to do to assure future generations a better world?*

If I were President, I would ask everyone concerned about the economy to read Jeremy Rifkin's book, *The Third Industrial Revolution*. This book challenges all of us to think in terms of the paradigm-shifting that is needed for tomorrow.

"Paradigm-shifting" is thinking outside the box. It is imagining completely new ways for things to be. It is not making a minimal shift, 5 or 10% this way or that. We are in a brand new ball game, and we need a new way to look at things.

Our economy looks like the work of an addict: multiple credit cards with big balances; borrowing from Peter to pay Paul; piling up debt; creditors knocking on the door; impending bankruptcy;

money deals being done out the back door. Always making excuses. Always some story as to where the money went.

Let's start with a simple proposition for an economic plan that is used by every sane American. *We are self-supporting, and we have a prudent reserve.* Period. We don't spend money we don't have, and we save something for a rainy day.

It's a simple principle.

We need to start with revising the tax code that was created by the 1% to serve the 1%'s need for even more money. You would think that a tax code specifying tax requirements for individuals and companies would be, say, a few pages long. Well, it turns out that our current tax code is 17,000 pages long. It was written by the 1% to give special breaks to thousands of corporations, special interests and God knows what else.

Our tax code should be understandable by every high school student who is studying civics.

If I were President, I would challenge the American people to put us to work. I'd go on national TV and say to the American public something like the following:

> *"My fellow Americans,*
>
> *I have a request. I'd like you to call your Congressperson tomorrow and tell them that you want them to get our financial house in order. I want you to remind them that they work for you, and if they don't perform, you will not vote for them.*
>
> *This is important, because Washington D.C. is full of men standing on every corner with bags of cash. Each time your Congressperson walks past, these dealers give buckets of cash to your guy. And you know where that's gotten us.*
>
> *I want each of the two parties to pick their ten best people. I want these 20 public servants to go to Camp David for no more than 30 days, and to come up with a bipartisan plan for our economy. The economic plan must include a tax code that is no longer than 25 pages (replacing the one that is now 17,000 pages) long. This plan would take away special breaks for corporations – like the one that allowed General Electric to pay no taxes on 4.6 billion dollars of profit made in 2010. It would restore the Glass-Steagall Act, levy a transaction tax on those who buy and sell millions of shares of stock per day, and create transparency in all transactions. This plan would remove all subsidies*

to corporations, like the one that gives Big Oil twenty-eight billion dollars a year, or the one that gives Big Food fourteen billion dollars a year to put lousy food in our school lunch programs. It would identify banks that are "too big to fail" and create a mechanism to break them up. And this plan would balance our budget and set up a prudent reserve to have on hand for a rainy day.

I want you to continue to make more noise than the guys on the corners with the cash, because I want Congress to unanimously and immediately (in 7 days or less) adopt the plan this group proposes, and I will immediately sign it into law.

This bill will certainly be imperfect, and will disrupt a lot of things, but it will be a start toward recovering America's fiscal integrity and restoring health to America's middle class.

Please, this is important. You really all need to email or call Congress each week or even every day. All of you!

Seriously! And they will listen — because you will not vote for them if they don't.

So, Americans, speak up! Raise your voices and go to the streets. Make our democracy work, for the sake of our children, our country, and the planet.

I will talk to you next week, and every week, and let you know how your elected officials are doing."

This new economic plan would fix our debt problem, our tax problem, and our spending problem. And this plan could be less than 40 pages in length. It would close corporate loopholes and eliminate unwise subsidies.

Additionally, I would ask each of us, every American, to "step up." We need to adjust all aspects of our money use, probably by no more than 5%. Wouldn't you gladly pay 5% more in taxes or get 5% less in entitlements if it meant that the economic system were fixed, and that it would ultimately lead to *much lower taxes and a sustainable and secure country and world?* My guess is that the stock market would soar, and the price of gold would drop, if we actually got our economic engine in gear and stopped mucking up the economic system with complex, contradictory, discriminatory, and anti-market regulations that are designed to make the wealthy even wealthier.

And I believe this 5% tax increase would only be temporary. We need a bloated government like we need another hole in our heads. Seriously! We have let our politicians create a huge bureaucracy to support their pet projects.

I would invite Jeremy Rifkin to meet with Congress, and myself, and all of our respective staff and help us envision a green economy. He has been advising the European Union on how to go green, create millions of jobs doing it, and possibly save the planet. This has to be the economy of the future. The carbon age is over. What Rifkin and the Europeans have been doing is making this a reality. The plan has been well thought out and makes sense. It is based on 5 pillars, as mentioned in my earlier chapter on energy:

1. Move from reliance on carbon-based fuel to sustainable and renewable energy.

2. Reconfigure buildings to become individual collectors of energy.

3. Install hydrogen and other technologies to store energy in each of these buildings.

4. Connect all of us in America to an intelligent grid, like the Internet, where we can all share energy and store energy.

5. Move our transportation fleet to electricity.

I would ask that we all meet once a month and rapidly implement his and others' visions of a sustainable, green energy policy. Rifkin has been working with the European Union for years, and Europe is far ahead of us. (Even China is marching past us!) While I applaud Europe's work, I know that America can move faster at what they are doing. When Americans put their mind to something, we don't mess around. We ended WWII, put men on the moon, and are leading the technological revolution. We just need to get our heads screwed on straight.

This new approach will create hundreds of thousands of business opportunities and millions of jobs. The question is: Can we pull it off before it's too late?

Additionally, I would convene the 400 wealthiest Americans, and I would respectfully ask them what they could do for America. I would start with the assumption that they are creative, good people at heart, and have simply gotten caught up in a dysfunctional system. I would invite them to see what they could come up with to help our country. I'm sure that they love America, and they have simply been enacting the American "success story." They would probably appreciate someone with vision giving their lives more meaning. One possibility might be for them to allocate some of their wealth to pay unemployed workers to plant trees – more trees, which will help reduce our CO_2 emissions. These brilliant thinkers are an untapped natural resource.

America's corporations currently are sitting on 2.5 trillion dollars that performs no function. Much of that money is parked offshore. We need to give these corporations a tax holiday to bring the money home, and tax incentives to keep their money here, and public recognition when they use their money to help save America. Imagine what that money could do.

Gandhi said, "We have enough for every man's need, but not enough for every man's greed."

If I were President, I would put a large sign on the lawn of the White House. The sign would show the changes in each citizen's share of America's net worth, debt, and prudent reserve. We need to understand that we are *each* responsible, and not surrender the reins of power to the 1% and let them have their way. We need to help America recover her financial sobriety.

That is what I would do. I'm sure that you, too, could come up with something that also makes much more sense than what the current leaders are doing.

We just need to find the courage and energy to stand up for America and the planet. Please, consider running for office. 90% of us think Congress is not getting the job done.

Sounds like a pretty big opening for some new blood.

13

DEFENSE AND FOREIGN POLICY

What would our defense policy look like if America's political system were not corrupt? What could change?

Let's start with a look at the name, "Secretary of Defense." We need such a person because nations can be mean and angry and dangerous. Some wars make sense. Fighting Germany in the 1940s did. Today's world can be dangerous. But does it need to always be this way? Sometimes having a military gets us in trouble.

I believe that our best defense is a great offense. An offense of morality, leadership, and sanity. We need to settle down and get our own house in order. My fantasy would be to live in a world where we did not even need to be defensive. Being defensive is *always* appropriate when danger is near. But what would it be like to live in a world that was safe? That would be my vision. To create a world that did not need armies and guns. Where countries, instead of fighting each other, worked cooperatively to save our planet and celebrate our diversity.

I believe that the primary focus of our species needs to be saving our planet.

We all need to come out of denial. We, you and I, are 100% responsible for our current political and environmental reality. Democracies are governments by the people. We each need to envision a sane world and then take action to manifest that – run for office, go to the streets, share our views online, attend political events, vote, etc.

Imagine yourself guiding us out of this mess. The following is what I would do. *What are you willing to do to assure future generations a better world?*

On day one of my presidency I would not change much regarding our foreign policy. The State Department is doing a good job, under the circumstances. I especially like how women leaders conducted the Libya event in 2011. Hillary Clinton, Susan Rice and their teams quietly, behind the scenes, worked with others to collaborate and integrate the use of military forces from several countries to protect Libya from a cruel dictator.

And the Secretary of Defense and his team have been doing a wonderful job as well, given the current situation. Unfortunately, we have put the fine men and women who serve in our military in harm's way. I would hope to get all nations to come together on the common problems that threaten all of our planet, rather than focusing on eradicating terrorists. Our planet is at risk, and that affects every one of us, in every nation. If we can see that we have a bigger problem, I think that we can focus on that and come together to form an international police force to deal with pockets of "out of control Chimpanzees." As it is now, many countries are acting like drunks with chips on their shoulders, leaving all of us frightened that they may "lose it" at any moment.

However, I have a question that none of us wants to face. Does anyone want our Department of Defense putting down their guns and shutting off our carbon supplies to save the Earth, because we were not smart enough to move to non-carbon-burning energy sources?

I hope it does not come to that. But Einstein may have been right, after all, when he questioned whether humans are smart enough to survive as a species.

As President, I would go to the United Nations and give a talk. I would hope that everyone on the planet could see the presentation. It would go something like this:

"Citizens of Earth: I am here to speak to you, not as the President of the United States, but as a fellow citizen of this small, blue ball called Earth.

I am here to talk about a problem that many of you know about, but many others of you may still be unaware of. What I'm talking about is the reality that Earth, our planet, is in trouble, and that affects all of us and all life around us.

For many decades we have been burning carbon, without paying much attention to the consequences. The reality is that our biosphere is very fragile, and we have been destroying it. Some of our scientists say that the situation is dire. Others say that we have a problem, but that it is not serious at this point. And there are those who want to believe that there is no problem.

I believe we have a problem, and we need to take seriously what science is telling us. We need to move toward policies that will eliminate this problem.

We can do this. We can do this, but it will take cooperation among all of us. We need to put our partisan differences aside. We are all citizens of Earth; Earth's air and water are not boundaried by nations' borders.

I call on the leaders of all countries. We must work together. We are the people's servants; it is our job to serve every person on Earth. We must act in unison and restore sanity to the governments of Earth. We must remember what Mahatma Gandhi said, "Earth has enough for every man's need, but not enough for every man's greed."

And I call on all the people. We need your help. We need you to peacefully stand up and remind all leaders whom we are pledged to serve.

It is time to put down the swords. It is time to see that we are all members of the species, Homo sapiens, *and to realize that our species is at risk of becoming extinct. All other concerns must be secondary.*

It is time for Americans to use less carbon and oil, to shift from reliance on fossil fuels to using more solar, wind, and electrical energy.

I will continue to speak to the other leaders and work to coordinate Earth's rescue efforts. This will be a massive effort, but I believe there is a gift in all of this.

In the past, we have acted crazily. We have pillaged, fought, raped and destroyed Nature. This crisis is forcing us to come together. This is good news.

Working together needs to be our priority.

I ask you, the citizens of Earth, to come together on this. I ask that all of us, every month, stand up and celebrate our humanity. We are all one species. At noon on the first Saturday of every month, I ask you to come together for two hours and sing and dance and pray and meditate and be with each other. I ask all of us to do this in order to bring awareness to this critical issue.

Other leaders and I will join you. Every month we will come to a new time zone and report to you how we are doing in our common effort. I will do this, to make the point that this is a global effort."

This is what *I* would do, if I were President.

14

POPULATION PLAN

When I read Paul Ehrlich's 1968 book, *The Population Bomb*, it terrified me. It made sense. We were multiplying like rats, and pooping in our cages. A few decades later, I listened to the siren song Big Business was singing. In effect, it was saying:

> *"Look, don't worry about the population-growth thing. We've got it handled. We have figured out a way to use science to improve on millions of years of God's work. We will rip up huge patches of nature, dam up great rivers, dig up gazillions of barrels of oil and use it to make fertilizer and other chemicals to dump on top of genetically modified corn and soybeans. We will then run this "food" through big chemical factories and squirt out substances that we will call food. We will add a lot of sugar, fat, and salt. Everyone will love it! It will be easy to feed everyone. It's handled, everybody! Chill out and go back to your TV, kick back, grab a beer and some snacks, and relax."*

Tom Freidman, author of *Hot, Flat and Crowded*, recently wrote: "What were we thinking? How did we not panic when the evidence was so obvious that we'd crossed some growth/climate/natural resource/population red lines all at once?"

He was referring to the spikes in food and energy prices, soaring population growth, tornadoes plowing through cities, unprecedented floods, record heat, displaced people, terrorism, and corrupt governments that are unable to address these problems.

The Earth's human population was two billion in 1920 and it will be fourteen billion in 2100. That's a seven-fold increase. America's population has tripled in the 20ᵗʰ century. From a population of 76 million in 1900, it grew to 281 million in 2000 and is continuing to grow at about 1.3% per year. By 2030, the population of America will be close to 400 million – almost 30% more than today. If, between 15 and 30 % of American children go to bed hungry now, what do you imagine the situation will be in 2030?

Our population was stable for a million years, until we started digging up coal, and then oil, and used these energy sources to produce more food. Today, 364,000 new babies are born every day. We are rapidly consuming more and more "wild" – wilderness and unharmed land – and within our children's lives most of it will be gone. The Trans-Amazon Highway is cutting through the center of the Amazon rainforests and obliterating the last great wilderness.

Today, you and I are part of a system that has brainwashed us to buy all the stuff we buy and to behave the way we do. We need to turn this around. We could do some *positive* brainwashing about the benefits of producing fewer children. Population growth has slowed in Western Europe. And many countries have, or will soon have, negative population growth. The more educated we become, the fewer babies we have. Generally, better-educated people recognize the emotional, financial, and other commitments that raising children entails. I think once everyone comes out of denial and sees the problem, we can move to the solution.

Many schools currently have a "Take a Baby Home Program" in place, but it needs to be greatly expanded. Right now some high school students are assigned a "baby" to take care of – an actual, baby-sized replica of a baby, with a computer chip that mimics a baby's sounds. They are tasked with giving up their lives for a weekend to take care of the baby. This "baby" requires constant feeding, holding, bathing, diaper-changing, and attending to. Lose focus for a moment and it screams! The computer chip records how well the teen is doing. These teens are amazed at how hard it is to care for a child. And they report that they are *very clear* that they don't want to have a kid any time soon! We would go a long way to reducing addiction, mental disorders, and burdens on society, if we eliminated unplanned pregnancies.

We would hope that all children are born to sane and mature adults. But sadly, many Americans are born to individuals who are not very mature. We need to address the underlying causes of immature adults having babies. These underlying causes include poverty, addiction, malnutrition, and poor education. When we are able to understand this and see that children are loved, fed, educated, and protected from neglect, abuse, and drugs, we will have made giant strides toward removing the underlying causes of unwanted babies.

We all need to come out of denial. We, you and I, are 100% responsible for our current political and environmental reality. Democracies are governments by the people. We each need to envision a sane world and then take action to manifest that – run for office, go to the streets, share our views online, attend political events, vote, etc.

Imagine yourself guiding us out of this mess. The following is what I would do. *What are you willing to do to assure future generations a better world?*

I would like all of us to visualize a population that lives in harmony with Earth, a population that has repaired this small blue ball.

I would create a cabinet post, Secretary of the Population, whose mandate would be to raise awareness of the population explosion, worldwide.

I would task this person with the following:

- Expand the "Take a Baby Home Program" to every school-aged child.
- Work with the media to raise awareness of the impact that people place on the planet.
- Work with the United Nations to raise awareness, around the world, of this problem and use our resources to expand the "Take a Baby Home Program" worldwide.
- Make birth control readily and freely available.
- Expand sex education to prevent unwanted pregnancies.

- Encourage the adoption of unplanned children.
- Encourage all nations to provide food, medical care, and education to all children.
- Support the end of wars and the development of educated, democratic populations.

Education should include:

- Parent education on what it entails to raise a baby to age 18: financially, emotionally, educationally, etc.
- What is the effect on the country's and the planet's resources of more mouths to feed?
- Consequences of malnutrition.
- Consequences of overcrowding.
- Contraception: if you don't want to become a parent, what are your choices?

My hope is that, given the right information, *Homo sapiens* might make it. We have produced democracy, science, and many other brilliant things. Reducing our population significantly should not be that hard. We need to prove Einstein wrong.

That would be my message. And my hope

15

FOOD

I was scared as I imagined publishing parts of this book. I talked to numerous lawyers and writers and friends. The next chapter, in particular, raised some necessary red flags. I assumed that freedom of speech was universal in America, and then I learned that I needed to understand the implications of words like "defamation" and "malicious intent" and "liability."

I learned what you will read in the next pages - that Oprah said on her program that she would not eat another hamburger, and was sued. Oprah's words cost her a million dollars in legal fees.

The Big Food industry is huge and does not want certain facts to be made public. As stated in this chapter, they have created laws in 17 states that make it a crime to criticize food. And they will sue, even if they can't win, knowing that it will cost whomever they sue a lot of money to defend themselves. The resulting chilling effect has almost prevented me from writing this chapter.

So, to you, Food Industry lawyers, I say this: Please don't sue me. All of the information regarding food in this chapter, and elsewhere in this book, has come from two documentaries: *Food, Inc.*, and *Forks Over Knives.* I have not independently verified the statements in these movies. I am simply reporting what I heard and saw in those films. I do not represent myself as an expert or an authority on food, diets, food production, medicine, or any other aspect of food.

My *personal* experience is clear. The further I get from what Big Food offers, the healthier I feel and the healthier I am. I choose my food today based on what I have learned from science and medicine, and my diet is almost entirely plant-based and free of processed foods. I try not to let the food propaganda of the 1% sway my food choices.

For a million years, our ancestors lived in harmony with nature. 10,000 years ago, some of our forefathers and mothers learned how to farm and raise animals. For the next 9,900 years, we continued to live in harmony with nature. Cancer, heart disease, diabetes, and strokes were rare or nonexistent. In the last one hundred years, our "brilliance" and our greed have put us on a trajectory that is *unsustainable.* We are now like the cartoon character, Wily Coyote, in *Roadrunner,* who has run off a cliff and has just realized that he's about to meet a tragic end.

Today in America we have a food policy that is not sane. We have greedy CEOs running multi-national Big Food Businesses. Big Food is bribing government officials to pass insane, destructive, and goofy laws that will net these companies even more money. The politicians get kickbacks to pay Big Media billions of dollars to run *1984*-like propaganda on TV, ads that castigate the "other side," endlessly trying to deflect the voter from seeing the corruption. On top of this, you and I pay billions of dollars in taxes to finance "Farm Subsidies" that allow Big Food to produce and sell sugar, fat, and salt-laden products at *below cost*, driving small, organic farmers out of business.

Why do Americans eat a lot of crap? One reason is that we are genetically programmed to overeat certain foods as part of our survival mechanism. For over two million years, our genome had little contact with sugar, fat, and salt. These items were very rare in nature. We sought out these nutrients because they were a source of rich, energy-dense sustenance. When we found them, we would overindulge, because they had survival value and we couldn't be sure we would ever find them again. Because of this genetic hardwiring, the average person can easily lose control and become addicted to sugar, fat, and salt-containing foods. Given a choice, the genome of *Homo sapiens* will gobble down a fast-food burger and fries (fat, salt, sugar) instead of fruits, grains, and vegetables, because we are hardwired to *know* that we may never find these foods again. Unless we take steps to stop what's going on in our food culture, this mess will get worse. It is just as easy to become addicted to these enticing foods as to drugs, and they are far more prevalent and available, especially to children.

We are genetically programmed to become addicted to what your politician has legislated to make ubiquitous! Our government's "social engineering" gives billions of dollars to multinational, processed-food-creating corporations, and then passes laws that make fat, salt, and sugar very cheap and very available! *Just like a drug dealer who gives away drugs to get you hooked.*

The chemically altered stuff that Big Food squirts out of their factories is called "food" and has addicted over a hundred million Americans, sickened millions of children, created a national obesity problem, and led to tens of millions of early deaths.

This rigged, corrupt, and immoral behavior on the part of Big Food and Big Government is completely wrong. They are slowly killing millions of Americans.

Here are some mind-blowing realities exposed in two recent movies, *Food, Inc.*, and *Forks Over Knives*. Both movies are well sourced and not news to healthy Americans and those who care about and understand the science of food. Some Americans probably already know most of this and will not be surprised. However, the majority of America has been duped. Big Food, our government, and a lazy Big Media have insanely perpetrated a heinous crime on Americans, and more egregiously, on our children.

- Fact: One in three American babies born after 2000 will get diabetes as a result of eating a diet rich in processed food.

- Fact: Over 30% of Americans have become obese following the diets approved by the "scientists" at the United States Department of Agriculture. (Many of these "scientists" work for, or are consultants to Big Food.)

- Fact: There are laws that make it a felony to criticize this drug-pushing scam. Criticize beef in Colorado, go to prison. There are actual laws in Colorado that say it is illegal to criticize beef. (Most industries are proud of their work. Why would Big Food need special laws, and thousands of lawyers standing by, to attack anyone who simply wants to see what is really going on?)

- Fact: Big Food and our "leaders" make it illegal to criticize any of our food! The following is from Wikipedia. "Food libel laws, also known as food disparagement laws and informally as veggie libel laws, are laws passed in 13 U.S. states that make it easier for food producers to sue their critics for libel. These 13 states include Alabama, Arizona, Colorado, Florida, Georgia, Idaho, Louisiana, Mississippi, North Dakota, Ohio, Oklahoma, South Dakota, and Texas. Many of the food-disparagement laws establish a lower standard for civil liability and allow for punitive damages and attorneys' fees for plaintiffs alone, regardless of the case's outcome."

- Fact: We spend 2.5 trillion dollars on healthcare (five times the defense budget). Treating chronic disease that our drug-dealing leaders are responsible for accounts for 75% of our healthcare costs. Our taxes would go way, way, way down if our leaders simply stopped subsidizing Big Food – simply stopped pushing fat, salt, and sugar.

- Fact: Plant-based diets, as opposed to animal-based diets, *can radically reduce, or even eliminate, obesity, heart disease, strokes, cancer, and diabetes.*

- Fact: The government fails to report the above information because government officials answer to Big Food. They don't want to talk about plant-based diets because it would expose the conspiracy that brings them billions of dollars. Big Food suppresses this information because of their greed. (And *we* gobble up their "food" because we are genetically wired to overeat fat, salt, and sugar. We are suckers for the "drug" they push.)

- Fact: It takes ten times the amount of oil to produce a calorie of animal-based food than it does to produce a calorie of plant-based food. (And more global heating.)

- Fact: The world's cattle, alone, eat enough grain to feed 8.7 billion people, nearly 2 billion more than the population on Earth. With almost 1 billion malnourished people across the globe, redirecting even a portion of the grain used to fatten cattle could feed every hungry mouth on the planet.

- Fact: According to a United Nations report, the livestock industry is a greater contributor to global warming than transportation or other industry! (A half-pound burger results in more carbon dioxide being produced than driving a car 10 miles.)

- Fact: 20% of the Amazon rainforest (an area the size of California) has been cleared and trashed to raise livestock, to support our Big Food and Big Government's push of a fat, salt, and sugar-rich diet on Americans.

- Fact: For every one-dollar, fast-food burger eaten, we pay close to $25 to treat the medical consequences. For every burger some poor person eats, we all end up paying much higher taxes. Big Food and our "leaders" get their cash up front, and we taxpayers get screwed with higher taxes and higher healthcare costs.

As noted above, in many states you cannot criticize food or the food industry or the food business. Be very careful, because if you do, you may be breaking a law and be sent to prison. It is very, very dangerous to criticize food. The oligarchy has us here. We all need to eat, and trillions of dollars are at stake. And President Obama, and your senator and representative have enabled, and are responsible, for this.

In addition to the laws that Big Food got Big Government to pass, thousands of lawyers working for Big Food will initiate frivolous lawsuits against anyone who *criticizes food!* These businesses have a lot to hide and are very defensive, and will aggressively attack us if we even try to see what they are doing.

Oprah Winfrey, the TV personality, after hearing that people were dying from eating E. coli-poisoned, fast-food burgers, said she would not eat another hamburger. Immediately, hordes of attorneys from Big Food came after her. It took thousands of hours and over a *million dollars* in attorneys' fees for Oprah to not go to prison. So, folks, do not criticize Big Food unless you have a spare million lying around to defend yourself, or are willing to risk going to prison.

I'm actually quite frightened that they will come after my family and me and we will be sued and lose everything for pointing out in this book what science already knows. To protect myself from Big Food's lawyers, I am going to hide behind two documentaries that have already done the research, *Food, Inc.* and *Forks Over Knives.*

From *Food, Inc.* comes the story of a middle-class Colorado mom who bought a hamburger for her son at a fast-food restaurant. Days later, her 2-year-old son, Kevin, died of E. coli poisoning from the contaminated burger. This fast-food, bad meat disaster had happened many times before, so this mother took steps to get our government to pass a law to protect us. This makes complete sense, except it turns out that our government protects us from the food industry about as well as it protects us from Wall Street or protects children from nicotine, i.e., they don't. Seven years after being introduced in Congress, "Kevin's Law" has yet to be passed.

Kevin's Law is officially known as the Meat and Poultry Pathogen Reduction and Enforcement Act of 2003. It was pretty straightforward. It authorized the Department of Agriculture inspectors to look for dangerous strains of E. coli in meat-processing factories. If they found any, they could shut the factory down until the pathogens were eliminated. After all, this bug was killing Americans. Big Food said that the law would impact "Economic Growth" and force up the price of hamburgers. The reality is that they don't want their costs to increase, and they are prioritizing cost over health. What Big Food also cares about is hiding what it's doing from the public.

Today, 90% of the meat we eat comes from cows that are fed not grass, but genetically modified corn and soybeans in "CAFOs" (Concentrated Animal Feeding Operations). In these huge setups, hidden away, thousands of cows stand ankle-deep in shit, eating chemically altered "food." Many of the workers in these plants are illegal immigrants bused from Mexico by government-enabled Big Business. The poor, shit-covered cows are shipped to top-secret slaughterhouses where more immigrants cut up cow carcasses for distribution to a genome (us) unable to resist overeating the end product (fat, salt, sugar).

(*Food, Inc.* reports that the feed-and-slaughter industry publicly advertises in Mexico to recruit illegal workers, and then buses these illegal aliens to American factories. They are violating the law, and our government officials *know this.* The Republicans support this practice, and the Democrats look the other way. Then, periodically, the government calls in the Immigration and Naturalization Service to *stage small arrests to make it look like they are doing something to stop this practice.*)

Immoral. Corrupt. They all need to go!

The press is our Fourth Estate, and even it is frightened to tell the truth about why it can't report this travesty.

Upton Sinclair published *The Jungle* in 1906. He pointed out the shocking conditions in Chicago's meatpacking industry and the corrupt officials who oversaw it. What we have now is much worse. Clearly the mainstream media is afraid to face Big Food and the government-enabled lawsuits.

I wonder what Big Food would not want us to know.

Every year our government gives billions of dollars to Big Food. Big Food is *Big.* I am going to simplify the following scenario. The majority of America's farmers are paid a lot of money to grow *only* corn and soybeans. These farmers are using oil-based, synthetic fertilizer, created by environment-destroying Big Chemical and Big Oil. Producing this fertilizer heats the planet, depletes our carbon, ruins the soil, and creates effluent that poisons our rivers and oceans. Government subsidizes this corn and soybean production so these crops can be grown below cost. Government and Big Food got together and planned this to prevent any competition from small farmers. The American Farmer is *gone!* The Republicans, the standard bearers for capitalism and small business, have been bought off, and in the last 50 years, have helped to *eliminate* small, family-run farms in America. These corn and soybean crops are genetically altered to prevent birds and bugs from surviving anywhere near them, which sterilizes giant swaths of our "fruited plains," killing Mother Earth and causing untold numbers of critters to become extinct. The corn and soybeans are then sent to giant, and nearly top-secret, factories where chemists, using massive amounts of oil, break down these genetically modified plants into a bunch of chemicals that are then chemically recombined to produce the base materials, that are then recombined again and packaged to look like *food.*

Just read the labels.

The majority of what is available in a supermarket is simply these recombined chemicals, packaged in a way that lures shoppers to buy them, and eat them, and causes Americans to become fat and sick. Obesity is skyrocketing. *One third of all people born in the United States after the year 2000 will develop diabetes and could die a horrible and early death.* Please reread that last sentence.

We created this! You and I. We elected these politicians who collude in this immoral and deadly process!

Your Senator, your Representative, your President made the laws and regulations that caused this. If asked, they will spew out some bullshit about how they are not responsible (others guy's fault) or what new agency they will appoint to address the problem. If they are not responsible, who the hell is?

(They all have to go! In 2012. All of them.)

This is insane. These greedy businesses are costing us billions! But worse than that, they are feeding us "food" that makes us sick and contributes to bankrupting Medicare. I would much rather pay more to buy food that did not cause cancer, diabetes, strokes or heart disease, or make kids sick and fat. Plus, this would go a long way toward fixing our financial system and saving the planet. *Our taxes and oil consumption would go way down if we stopped this charade.*

Think about it. Just look around. Look at all the obese people. Obese people see a lot of doctors, take a lot of medicines and go to a lot of hospitals. Who pays for this? Medicare, Medi-Cal, Social Security, etc. But there is another, saner approach. Recovery from food addiction. I know old people who changed their eating habits and are now healthy and running, swimming, biking in their 70s and 80s. *They have very low, or even no, medical costs!*

In effect, Big Food is saying; "Sorry, we really don't care about the consumer. We don't care about children. We don't care about future economic costs. We have a thing going on here, and we don't want to talk about it." Seriously, they don't want us to see what goes on in their factories.

And we have allowed this. We passively stand by. We all need to wake up and put sane people in charge. If we randomly picked a bunch of farmers who are using sustainable practices and put them in charge of our food, we would save many millions of lives and many billions of dollars! How many Americans died in World War II? Just soldiers alone, over 100,000. How many died in Vietnam? 60,000. How many died in Iraq? 5,000 and counting. Our current, criminal Food Policy is killing more people every year than the number of Americans who died in all of those wars. Big Food and our bought-off leaders are responsible for millions of very messy, early deaths, every year.

Look what happened when Michelle Obama just mentioned that our kids should eat healthier food. She touched the third rail. *Can't talk about that!* Big Business and bought-off Republicans attacked her. Did these elected Republicans, knowing that their own children are being put at a disadvantage by fast food, stand up for science and morality and "what's right," and the future of their children? No. Did the Democrats stand up and support this simple and obvious inquiry about healthy eating? Of course not; they, too, get millions from Big Food. I wept as I watched Michelle Obama, an advocate for children, being attacked by a corrupt system. What politicians, Big Business, and the media that support our current sick system, did was wrong. Plain and simple.

Rush Limbaugh is right. The *Lame Stream Media* is not sane. 99% of the media did not go ballistic at the insanity of Big Business and Big Government's attack on Michelle's simple but sane views promoting healthy eating for children. Big Media enables the status quo. Julian Assange, the founder of Wikileaks, has a point: Big Media is in bed with Big Business and Big Government.

We are learning that sugar, like tobacco, kills us. Simple carbohydrates containing sugar are beneficial when combined with the thousands of other micronutrients found in *real food, like fruits and vegetables, legumes, nuts, and seeds.* But the sugar, and fake sugar, ingested in sodas, candy, cereal, processed bread, canned vegetables, processed meats, and a thousand other products, is *not real.* It is manufactured. Ingesting sugar can lead to cancer, obesity, diabetes, heart disease, strokes, developmental delays, and early death. Not only can it lead to those diseases, but also it is the reason that one third of children born today are expected to develop diabetes. Processed sugar, in all its varieties, is a bad chemical. But many Americans are addicted to it − and peddling this chemical makes billions of dollars for Big Business. And millions of dollars get passed on to the leaders, who rig the system.

Now you can see why our government subsidizes sugar!

Robert Lustig, M.D., specialist in pediatric hormone disorders at the University of California, San Francisco, gave a lecture that has gone viral on the Web. Over 1.4 million people have watched it. If you care about saving America, I implore you to watch one of our leading doctors "tell it like it is." The video is called, *Sugar: The Bitter Truth.* The link to the YouTube video is: http://www.youtube.com/watch?v=dBnniua6-oM)

In his presentation, Dr. Lustig talks about high fructose corn syrup, which Big Food erroneously labels "food," and adds to almost every food product found in today's supermarkets. Dr. Lustig calls sugar a "toxin," and a "poison." Five times he calls sugar "evil." He calls high fructose corn syrup "the most demonized additive known to man."

Today, your President, Senator, and Representative are signing off on selling more sugar to children, one third of whom will get diabetes.

"Sustainable farming" is how we have farmed since the beginning of agriculture. Our cows ate grass and fertilized the grass with their poop. Millions of critters, large and small, lived in harmony, nearby. When it rained, nature automatically cleaned everything up. *Zero carbon footprints.* This has to be our goal if we are going to keep our planet alive. We must remove the insane leaders who allowed Big Farm to destroy our land. We must restore Mother Earth.

This is the Big Food equation:

Money + Government Corruption + Genetic Vulnerability	=	Addiction that leads to massive killing of Americans.

We are getting fatter and fatter. Think about it. We adults may choose to kill ourselves. *But our children!* Shame on us! Aren't we also genetically programmed to protect children *with our lives?* How could we allow public schools to feed our children food that compromises their health? How could we allow schools to have vending machines that sell these addictive substances? And how take our children to fast-food outlets? And bring home mountains of processed sugar and high fructose corn syrup? We may not have known the science behind overeating, but haven't we noticed our kids getting fatter and sicker and questioned whether what they ate played a role?

Big Business's Addiction to Money + Big Government's Addiction to Power + Human Vulnerability to Overeat Fat, Salt, Sugar + Psychological Defense of Denial = Proving Einstein correct!

We need to get rid of the corrupt politicians and elect wise leaders who will make *real food* a part of our lives.

> We all need to come out of denial. We, you and I, are 100% responsible for our current political and environmental reality. Democracies are governments by the people. We each need to envision a sane world and then take action to manifest that – run for office, go to the streets, share our views online, attend political events, vote, etc.
>
> Imagine yourself guiding us out of this mess. The following is what I would do. *What are you willing to do to assure future generations a better world?*

If I were President, I would ask everyone to watch the movies *Food, Inc.* and *Forks Over Knives.*

I would expect to pass Kevin's Law.

I would request that all members of the Senate, Congress, and the Administration, within 90 days after taking office, and every six months thereafter, visit the CAFOs cow, chicken, and pig factories, the food processing plants and the slaughterhouses, and see the effluent (shit) that flows from these concentration camps. I would visit them myself, with the press. We need to turn the lights on!

Next, in a careful unwinding, I would take all the money going to multi-national Big Farm corporations and give it to sustainable and organic farming. For the last 10,000 years, farming has been an honorable occupation. Some of the money we now spend to produce sugar, we can use to hire the unemployed to grow food. Giant agribusiness needs to be replaced by millions of small farms. These farms will thrive, because our new leaders will help educate all of us on the basics of raising food. Our government now artificially subsidizes certain food industries. We need to factor in the true costs of real food. We now have dollar burgers and pay three dollars a pound for broccoli. I would move the subsidies to healthy food production and away from manufacturing food that leads to poor health.

I would expose the practice of giving billions of dollars of your money to put cheap heroin on the streets that will addict your kids. Oops, I mean $C_{12}H_{22}O_{11}$, also known as high fructose corn syrup. (Actually, heroin kills 7,000 people a year. High fructose corn syrup has killed, and will kill, millions! We get *so* upset at heroin dealers, when the sugar industry is far, far, far more deadly!)

I would propose a rapid, but organized, unwinding of all farm subsidies, as they exist now. I would propose using some of the money saved from discontinuing subsidized farming to educate Americans about sustainable farming. The money saved from ending subsidies would lower our taxes, or go to subsidize the creation of millions of small farms (giving the unemployed still another opportunity for work). I propose that we treat sugar as the addictive chemical that it is. Sugar will be legal, but like other addictive substances, it will be regulated, and it will be taxed, and the revenue from taxes will be used to pay for education and the treatment of food addiction. Just like with other addictive substances, parents will keep sugar away from children. The goal would be to make healthy food available to everyone and to get government out of the process, except when it can contribute to the general good, as in education and treatment for food addiction.

I would ask all students, teachers, government officials, parents, doctors, therapists, and anyone who eats high fructose corn syrup to watch Robert Lustig's YouTube video, *Sugar: The Bitter Truth*. http://www.youtube.com/watch?v=dBnniua6-oM)

I would change the name of the Secretary of Agriculture to the Secretary of Food. I would direct this individual to remove all Big Food employees, or anyone who worked with Big Food, from government positions.

I would ask former President Clinton to share his personal story of regaining health as a result of moving to a plant-based diet. Remarkable things happen when we move from an animal-based diet to a plant-based diet. Bill Clinton's story is just one of these remarkable transformations. His "fast food" diet was in large part responsible for the coronary problems he developed that eventually led to his needing heart surgery. At the request of his doctors, and his daughter, he switched to a plant-based diet, lost excess weight, and today reports that his health is vastly improved. I would consider offering him the job of Secretary of Food.

I would review all government agencies and programs related to agriculture and food. These employees have created, enabled, or ignored this unbelievable nightmare! I would eliminate any grants to science or universities unless they focused on the solution. They have all been complicit in enabling this insane process. I would initiate a national dialogue about sustainable farming, organic farming, and permaculture. The goal would be to provide healthy food to every child *and to collectively celebrate the return of Mother Nature. We do have enough for every person's need, just not for every person's greed . . . for more and more and more.*

16

EDUCATION

All of us are saddened when we think about how our country manages education.

We see the bumper stickers:

> *"It will be a great day when our schools get all the money they need and the Air Force has to hold a bake sale to buy a bomber."*

Children need to be our first priority. Each of us becomes the person we are because of what happened in the critical, first 18 months of our lives. And the next critical three years. And every year, until we become adults. Every successful mammal prioritizes childcare, even at the risk of being killed to protect his or her young.

Most folks don't understand the stressors placed on today's kids. Children today live in a world where electronic screens seduce them away from nature, and play, and contact with other humans. They are growing up in a nation that has destroyed most of their wilderness. They hear that we have screwed up the economy and that we will leave them with the bill. And then they hear that the planet is at risk, and that their clueless parents are "asleep at the wheel" and failing to notice the unfolding tragedy. They text each other, on average, over one hundred times a day. And a recent report says that 70% of them get texts from their hovering, helicopter parents *while they are in class*!

If we care about children, we need to care about their teachers. Sadly, we are misguided here. We need to give teachers better salaries and allocate more funds to school programs. Nationwide, we are cutting back on field trips, sports, marching bands, art, and other activities that many of us older folks so loved when we were in school. And in higher education. California, for instance, used to have one of the best college systems in the land. And it was afford-able. Now it is in financial trouble, tuitions are rising, classes are closing, and kids are not getting the education and training they need for our nation to succeed in this technological era.

We need to get our priorities straight.

> We all need to come out of denial. We, you and I, are 100% responsible for our current political and environmental real-ity. Democracies are governments by the people. We each need to envision a sane world and then take action to mani-fest that – run for office, go to the streets, share our views online, attend political events, vote, etc.
>
> Imagine yourself guiding us out of this mess. The fol-lowing is what I would do. *What are you willing to do to assure future generations a better world?*

If I were President, I would ask all educators to read Jeremy Rifkin's book, *The Third Industrial Revolution*. This book challenges all of us to think in terms of the paradigm shift that is needed for tomorrow.

I would encourage all of us to take a look at this. We know that there are bureaucracies that suck up money. We know that there are calcified unions that protect uninspired teachers from being chal-lenged to hone their skills and learn new approaches. We have a ton of recent graduates who are unemployed and a lot of retired people who would have a lot to offer as teachers.

We need a "Sputnik Moment" in education to bring about Rifkin's vision of *The Third Industrial Revolution*, which I talk about in other parts of this book. We need to inspire all of us to imagine what we can give to the education system. We need to shake this up. America's education paradigm needs to become more like Steve Jobs's company, Apple. Apple had no committees. None. People col-laborated, brainstormed, and worked towards "what Steve wanted."

We need inspired leaders to lead us. If I were President, I would find educators with vision and then give them what they needed to make their visions a reality. Michael J. Sandel, the "rock star" professor from Harvard, is such a leader. He might make a great Secretary of Education. Imagine that we gave him a big chunk of the defense budget, got the federal government out of the way, got the unions out of the way, put all the textbooks on iPads, and aimed kids toward a relevant education.

WHAT'S NEXT?

What does each of us, as an American, choose to do?

What's next is for each of us, as individuals, to claim the power we have, the power that was given to us by our founders: the power to vote. Using this power – and holding our candidates to the standards I have proposed here, and getting money out of politics – is the necessary next step. Once we have exercised this power, we can begin to come together to make the changes necessary to create a functioning government, and begin the hard work of saving the environment and the planet.

This book encourages each of us to run for office in order to help restore democracy and sanity to a system that has become badly unbalanced by undemocratic election laws, laws that have enabled the election of unethical leaders who have failed to serve us.

We can do better, and, for the sake of both our planet and the generations to come, I hope that many Americans will make the decision to stand up and take action. I hope that many Americans will choose to run for office, write a book, start a blog, go to the streets, contribute to candidates and to movements, and participate in social change.

In this last year, I have taken most of these actions. In the process, I have discovered that a lot of people are doing similar things. It seems that there is a collective unconscious that is compelling many of us to act. I find this exciting and hopeful. I'm reminded of what Peggy Noonan, the conservative columnist for the *Wall Street Journal*, wrote in her column on October 14, 2011:

"And people have a sense that nothing's going to get better unless something big is done, some fundamental change is made in our financial structures. It won't be small-time rejiggering – a 5% cut in this tax, a 3% reduction in that program – that will get us out of this."

I believe we need to wake up to the reality that we are at the cusp of a new paradigm, one that celebrates the restoration of democracy and the healing of our planet.

We have examples in our history of people gathering peacefully to promote a cause.

I remember the free-spirited attitude of hippies. When we gathered or marched, we would bring flowers to give to the police! It was so inspiring to see everyone with big smiles, including the police, many of whom were carrying those flowers! We knew how to gather together and have fun. Boy, did we!

There is another group of Americans who, for decades, has been gathering in the thousands and having a wonderful, loving, and fun time. Each year during the week before Labor Day, fifty thousand people congregate at the Burning Man Festival in Black Rock City, Nevada. This in an intentional community that builds a whole city in days, complete with an airport, has a *massive* love-in and art festival, and then, seven days later, takes it all down, leaving behind *not one scrap of litter!* The Federal Government oversees this event, and members of half-a-dozen police jurisdictions wander peacefully among the people. *Nearly everyone, including the police, has fun.*

Then there is the Buddhist community that has, for centuries, quietly and peacefully demonstrated against injustices. You can depend on them to be peaceful. This is another group of individuals that has a wonderful reputation with police departments.

I propose that these three groups, old hippies, Burning Man folks, and Buddhists, become our mentors, our guides. These people know how to be peaceful, implement change, and have fun. These folks exhibit Bonobo-like behavior. *Being a jerk just creates more jerks.* There will always be a few people in these gatherings who will have "bad "trips (they almost always had been using drugs or alcohol). Back in the 60s, Bill Graham and Dr. David Smith of the Haight Ashbury Free Clinic knew how to handle this. They had doctors and nurses wandering among the crowds, attending to those who were having a bad time.

There will be people who will have a problem with this, I know. There are those who are threatened by the idea of change. Many are attached to one party or another and will feel very upset at the idea of their party's organization being usurped and bypassed. It will be important to welcome everyone into the movement and not engage in any conflict; simply walk away from any vexations. We are respectful and never, ever argue or become contentious. We will be modeling for others what sanity looks like. We will always cooperate with the police and leave our meeting area cleaner that it was before we arrived.

There are many on the far right and far left who are publicly active. Actually, I would appreciate that you not join us for a few months. My experience is that the fringes, while well meaning, are sometimes more interested in "fighting the problem" than "finding the solution." I know you mean well, but in the initial stage, we are gathering those who clearly see that *everyone* has been wrong, and that fundamental change is necessary. We need the sane and solid middle of America, the 20% of the voters, 40,000,000 of us, to make a decision to stand up for the planet and the children, and to come together to work toward the solution.

I trust us. I trust Americans. We have a rich heritage of doing the right thing. Today what is new and different is the Internet and instant communication. Suddenly anyone can talk to anyone. We have the means to communicate any message, worldwide, in seconds. We are in a different paradigm and we simply need to accept that reality. Once we do, we see how much power we have as individuals.

Are you ready?

I say, "Let's roll!"

REFERENCES

Abramoff, Jack. *Capitol Punishment: The Hard Truth About Washington Corruption From America's Most Notorious Lobbyist*. Washington, DC: WND Books, 2011.

Alexander, Michelle, *The New Jim Crow: Mass Incarceration in the Age of Colorblindness*. New York: The New Press, 2012.

Blackmon, Douglas, *Slavery by Another Name: The Re-Enslavement of Black Americans from the Civil War to World War II*. New York: Anchor Books, 2009.

Brown, Stephanie and Virginia Lewis, *The Alcoholic Family in Recovery: A Developmental Model*. New York: Guilford Press, 1998.

Alcoholics Anonymous, New York: Works Publishing, Inc., 1939. (Commonly referred to as the Big Book, or the Big Book of AA).

Campbell, T. Colin et al., *The China Study: The Most Comprehensive Study of Nutrition Ever Conducted and The Startling Implications for Diet, Weight Loss, and Long-term Health*. Dallas, Texas: Benbella Books, 2005.

De Waal, Frans, *Our Inner Ape: A Leading Primatologist Explains Why We Are Who We Are*. New York: Riverhead Books, 2005.

Ehrlich, Paul, *The Population Bomb*. San Francisco, California: Sierra Club/Ballantine Books, 1968.

Esselstyn, Rip, *The Engine 2 Diet: The Texas Firefighter's 28-Day Save-Your-Life Plan that Lowers Cholesterol and Burns Away the Pounds*. New York: Wellness Central, 2009.

Food, Inc. (Movie), 2009. Directed by Robert Kenner and produced by Robert Kenner and Elise Pearlstein.

Forks Over Knives (Movie), 2011. Directed by Lee Fulkerson and produced by Brian Wendel, John Curry and Allison Boon.

Friedman, Thomas L., *Hot, Flat and Crowded: Why We Need a Green Revolution – and How It Can Renew America*. New York: Farrar, Straus and Giroux, 2008.

Goleman, Daniel, *Emotional Intelligence: Why It Can Matter More Than IQ*. New York: Bantam Books, 1997.

Lessig, Lawrence, *Republic, Lost: How Money Corrupts Congress – and a Plan to Stop It*. New York: Twelve Publishers, 2011.

Lewis, Michael, *The Big Short: Inside the Doomsday Machine*. New York: W.W. Norton & Co., 2011.

Linden, David, *The Compass of Pleasure: How Our Brains Make Fatty Foods, Orgasm, Exercise, Marijuana, Generosity, Vodka, Learning, and Gambling Feel So Good*. New York: Viking, 2011.

Prud'homme, Alex, *The Ripple Effect*. New York: Scribners, 2011.

Rifkin, Jeremy, *The Third Industrial Revolution*. New York: Palgrave Macmillan, 2011.

ABOUT THE AUTHOR

Larry Fritzlan is a Licensed Marriage and Family Therapist, a Certified Addiction Specialist, and a Board Registered Interventionist. He is founder and director of Larry Fritzlan Recovery Services, a family-based outpatient drug rehab program for teens and young adults in Corte Madera, California. He specializes in doing interventions from a family systems perspective. He lives in Mill Valley, California with his wife, Avis Rumney. He is a candidate for Representative to the U.S. Congress from California's 2nd Congressional District, which includes the counties of Marin, Sonoma, Mendocino, Humboldt, Trinity and Del Norte.